*Terry N...*
BLA...
The Programm...

Tony Attwood, the Guide compiler, has been the resident composer/teacher at the Cockpit Theatre in London, Senior Lecturer in Music at Dartington College of Arts in Devon and now runs his own company, Hamilton House Publishing. He has written on topics as diverse as the radio industry and the problems facing British football. Recent works include the currently bestselling school text book for CSE and O Level music students, *Music From Scratch*, and a series of songbooks in which rock hits are arranged for school classrooms. He is also the publisher of two trade journals *Radio Directory* and *TV Directory* and editor of the *What's New Guide to Transport Cafés*. His desire to compile *The Blake's 7 Programme Guide* came simply from his total devotion to the series. He lives in Northamptonshire with his wife and their two daughters.

*Terry Nation's*

# BLAKE'S 7
## The Programme Guide

*Compiled by Tony Attwood*

## A TARGET BOOK

*published by*
the Paperback Division of
W. H. ALLEN & Co. Ltd

A Target Book
Published in 1983
by the Paperback Division of
W. H. Allen & Co. Ltd
A Howard and Wyndham Company
44 Hill Street, London W1X 8LB

First published in Great Britain by W. H. Allen & Co. Ltd, 1982

Text copyright © Tony Attwood 1982
Format copyright © Lynsted Park Enterprises Limited 1978

Printed in Great Britain by
Hunt Barnard Printing Ltd, Aylesbury, Bucks

ISBN 0 426 19449 7

This book is sold subject to the condition that it shall
not, by way of trade or otherwise, be lent,
re-sold, hired out or otherwise circulated without the
publisher's prior consent in any form of
binding or cover other than that in which it is published
and without a similar condition including this
condition being imposed on the subsequent purchaser.

# *CONTENTS*

*Special thanks to all the following:*

CHRIS BOUCHER
PAUL DARROW
SARAH EDWARDS
ROGER HANCOCK
SUSAN HESSE
MICHAEL KEATING
VERE LORRIMER
PETER TUDDENHAM

# Introduction
## by Terry Nation

The eminent lexicographers of the Oxford Dictionaries give a good deal of space to the definition of the word 'idea'. Philosophers, including Plato, Descartes, Locke and Kant have all contributed their learning in search for its meaning. Despite this wealth of erudition, I have still to find a satisfactory explanation for the word. It may be that the genesis of an 'idea' is an impossible history to write. I suspect that it is the coming together of thousands of fragmentary images, experiences, sounds, memories, all seemingly unrelated. When they combine, you suddenly have an 'idea'.

I mention my concern about the word because I am unable to honestly answer a question that is frequently asked. 'Where did you get the idea for . . . ?' The sentence ends with the title of a play or book or television series. 'Blake's 7' is the most recent subject of the inquiry. Try as I might, I cannot pin down its origins. I know only that the 'idea' has a wonderful talent for manifesting itself at the moment of greatest need. This is sometimes mistakenly called 'a flash of inspiration'. More accurately it is the product of desperation. Clearly, this was the case at my meeting at the BBC. We had discussed a number of projects which excited none of us. The interview was drawing to a close when I surprised myself by starting to detail a new science fiction adventure. 'It is set in the third century of the second calendar,' I explained. 'A group of criminals is being transported to a prison planet. Under the leadership of a wrongly convicted patriot, they escape and get hold of a super spacecraft, then begin to wage war against the evil forces of the Federation.' 'Have you got a title?' someone asked. ' "Blake's 7" ' I replied without hesitation. When I left the BBC that day I had a commission to write a pilot script and the bewildered feeling that once again I could not trace the source of the idea.

At the time of this writing the series has run for four years. A highly talented team of producers, writers, actors and technicians conspired together to make the programme an award-winning success that is seen around the world. The series has a huge and devoted audience and has become a cult with many of its followers.

I think I know what 'Blake's 7' is now, but at the beginning I had no idea.

*Los Angeles*
*April 1982*

# Prologue

Between January 1978 and December 1981 the BBC broadcast 52 episodes of 'Blake's 7'. The final episode was seen by over 10 million people, a figure which, although stunning in itself, is made all the more remarkable by the fact that it was achieved despite the programme being broadcast at the same time as the top ITV audience-catcher, 'Coronation Street'.

'Blake's 7' grabbed the public imagination in a way that only a handful of programmes had ever done before. Letters poured in to the BBC throughout the series. After each season of 13 programmes, hundreds of viewers offered solutions to the crises created in each final episode. By 1981 at least ten fan clubs existed in Britain alone, along with a 'Blake's 7' magazine selling 40,000 copies a month. Invitations to the actors to do everything from appearing at conventions to lecturing to students at Cambridge University have continued to arrive every day.

'Blake's 7' represented a unique attempt in the UK to mount a serious space futures serial. It presented heroes who were not invincible and escapades which were all the more plausible because they didn't always work. As early as the second series one of the leading characters, Gan, was killed off during a futile raid on the Federation's nerve centre. Cally died after an explosion caused by the arch-enemy Servalan. And Blake – if he wasn't dead before – was most certainly killed by Avon in the very last episode of all. This book commemorates one of the most important developments in television drama for over a decade. Thanks must go to everyone involved.

# Cast Listings

Avon: Paul Darrow
Blake: Gareth Thomas
Cally (series ABC only): Jan Chappell
Dayna (CD): Josette Simon
Gan (AB): David Jackson
Jenna (AB): Sally Knyvette
Orac: Peter Tuddenham
Servalan: Jacqueline Pearce
Slave (D): Peter Tuddenham
Soolin (D): Glynis Barber
Tarrant (CD): Steven Pacey
Travis (A): Stephen Greif
Travis (B): Brian Croucher
Vila: Michael Keating
Zen (ABC): Peter Tuddenham

These characters appeared regularly in 'Blake's 7', hence only additional characters are featured in the following lists. Transmission dates refer to the first showing of the episode in the United Kingdom.

# SERIES A

Author: Terry Nation
Series Script Editor: Chris Boucher
Series Producer: David Maloney

## 1. THE WAY BACK, transmitted Monday 2nd January 1978

Director: Michael Briant

Foster: Robert Beatty
Ravella: Gillian Bailey
Richie: Alan Butler
Tarrant: Jeremy Wilkin
Ven Glynd: Robert James
Dr Havant: Peter Williams
Alta Morag: Susan Field
Arbiter: Margaret John
Clerk of Court: Rodney Figaro
Computer Operator: Nigel Lambert
Guard: Garry McDermott
Varon: Michael Halsey
Maja: Pippa Steel

## 2. SPACE FALL, transmitted Monday 9th January 1978

Director: Pennant Roberts

Leylan: Glyn Owen
Raiker: Leslie Schofield
Artix: Norman Tipton
Teague: David Hayward
Krell: Brett Forrest
Nova: Tom Kelly
Dainer: Michael McKenzie
Garton: Bill Weston

## 3. CYGNUS ALPHA, transmitted Monday 16th January 1978

Director: Vere Lorrimer

Vargas: Brian Blessed
Kara: Pamela Salem
Arco: Peter Childs
Selman: David Ryall
Laran: Robert Russell
Leylan: Glyn Owen
Artix: Norman Tipton

## 4. TIME SQUAD, transmitted Monday 23rd January 1978

### Director: Pennant Roberts

Aliens: Tony Smart, Mark McBride, Frank Henson

## 5. THE WEB, transmitted Monday 30th January 1978

### Director: Michael Briant

Saymon: Richard Beale
Geela: Ania Marson
Novara: Miles Fothergill

The Decimas: Deep Roy,
Gilda Cohen, Izmet Hassam,
Marcus Powell, Molly
Tweedley, Willie Sheara

## 6. SEEK-LOCATE-DESTROY, transmitted Monday 6th February 1978

### Director: Vere Lorrimer

Prell: Peter Craze
Bercol: John Bryans
Rontane: Peter Miles

Rai: Ian Oliver
Escon: Ian Cullen
Eldon: Astley Jones

## 7. MISSION TO DESTINY, transmitted Monday 13th February 1978

### Director: Pennant Roberts

Kendall: Barry Jackson
Sara: Beth Morris
Mandrian: Stephen Tate
Sonheim: Nigel Humphreys

Grovane: Carl Forgione
Pasco: John Leeson
Levett: Kate Coleridge
Rafford: Brian Capron

Dortmunn: Stuart Fell

## 8. DUEL, transmitted Monday 20th February 1978

### Director: Douglas Camfield

Sinofar: Isla Blair

Giroc: Patsy Smart

Mutoid: Carol Royle

### 9. PROJECT AVALON, transmitted Monday 27th February 1978

Director: Michael Briant

Avalon: Julia Vidler
Chevner: David Bailie
Mutoid: Glynis Barber

Scientist: John Baker
Terloc: John Rolfe
Guards: David Sterne, Mark Holmes


### 10. BREAKDOWN, transmitted Monday 6th March 1978

Director: Vere Lorrimer

Kayn: Julian Glover
Farren: Ian Thompson
Renor: Christian Roberts


### 11. BOUNTY, transmitted Monday 13th March 1978

Director: Pennant Roberts

Sarkoff: T. P. McKenna
Tyce: Carinthia West
Tarvin: Mark Zuber

Cheney: Mark York
Amagon Guard: Derrick Branche


### 12. DELIVERANCE, transmitted Monday 20th March 1978

Directors: David Maloney, Michael Briant

Meegat: Suzan Farmer
Ensor: Tony Caunter
Maryatt: James Lister


### 13. ORAC, transmitted Monday 27th March 1978

Director: Vere Lorrimer

Ensor: Derek Farr
First Phibian: James Muir
Second Phibian: Paul Kidd

# SERIES B

Series Script Editor: Chris Boucher
Series Producer: David Maloney

1. **REDEMPTION,** transmitted Tuesday 9th January 1979
Author: Terry Nation
Director: Vere Lorrimer

Alta One: Sheila Ruskin      Alta Two: Harriet Philpin
Norm One: Roy Evans

2. **SHADOW,** transmitted Tuesday 16th January 1979
Author: Chris Boucher
Director: Jonathan Wright Miller

Bek: Karl Howman            The Enforcer: Archie Tew
Hanna: Adrienne Burgess     The Chairman: Vernon
Largo: Derek Smith            Dobtcheff

3. **WEAPON,** transmitted Tuesday 23rd January 1979
Author: Chris Boucher
Director: George Spenton-Foster

Fen: Kathleen Byron         Carnell: Scott Fredericks
Coser: John Bennett         The Officer: Graham
Rashel: Candace              Simpson
  Glendenning

4. **HORIZON,** transmitted Tuesday 30th January 1979
Author: Allan Prior
Director: Jonathan Wright Miller

Ro: Darien Angadi           Selma: Souad Faress
The Kommissar: William      Assistant Kommissar: Brian
  Squire                      Miller
Chief Guard: Paul Haley

5. **PRESSURE POINT,** transmitted Tuesday 6th February
1979
Author: Terry Nation
Director: George Spenton-Foster

Kasabi: Jane Sherwin      Arle: Alan Halley
Veron: Yolande Palfrey      Berg: Martin Connor
Mutoid: Sue Bishop

6. **TRIAL,** transmitted Tuesday 13th February 1979
Author: Chris Boucher
Director: Derek Martinus

Samor: John Savident      Par: Kevin Lloyd
Bercol: John Bryans      Lye: Graham Sinclair
Rontane: Peter Miles      Guard Commander: Colin Dunn
Thania: Victoria Fairbrother      Zil: Claire Lewis

7. **KILLER,** transmitted Tuesday 20th February 1979
Author: Robert Holmes
Director: Vere Lorrimer

Bellfriar: Paul Daneman      Bax: Michael Gaunt
Gambril: Colin Farrell      Tynus: Ronald Lacey
Tak: Colin Higgins      Wiler: Morris Barry

8. **HOSTAGE,** transmitted Tuesday 27th February 1979
Author: Allan Prior
Director: Vere Lorrimer

Space Commander:      Joban: Kevin Stoney
  Andrew Robertson      Ushton: John Abineri
Mutoid: Judith Porter      Molok: James Coyle
Inga: Judy Buxton

9. **COUNTDOWN,** transmitted Tuesday 6th March 1979
Author: Terry Nation
Director: Vere Lorrimer

Tronos: Geoffrey Snell
Selson: Robert Arnold
Provine: Paul Shelley
Ralli: Lindy Alexander

Del Grant: Tom Chadbon
Arrian: Nigel Gregory
Vetnor: Sidney Kean
Cauder: James Kerry

## 10. VOICE FROM THE PAST, transmitted Tuesday 13th March 1979
### Author: Roger Parkes
### Director: George Spenton-Foster

Glynd: Richard Bebb
Governor Le Grand:
  Frieda Knorr

Nagu: Martin Read

## 11. GAMBIT, transmitted Tuesday 20th March 1979
### Author: Robert Holmes
### Director: George Spenton-Foster

Krantor: Aubrey Woods
Toise: John Leeson
Docholli: Denis Carey
Chenie: Nicolette Roeg

Croupier: Sylvia Coleridge
Cevedic: Paul Grist
Jarriere: Harry Jones
Zee: Michael Halsey

The Klute: Deep Roy

## 12. THE KEEPER, transmitted Tuesday 27th March 1979
### Author: Allan Prior
### Director: Derek Martinus

Gola: Bruce Purchase
Rod: Shaun Curry
Tara: Freda Jackson

Old Man: Arthur Hewlett
Fool: Cengiz Saner
Patrol Leader: Ron Tarr

## 13. STAR ONE, transmitted Tuesday 3rd April 1979
### Author: Chris Boucher
### Director: David Maloney

Lurena: Jenny Twigge
Stot: David Webb
Parton: Gareth Armstrong
Durkim: John Bown
Marcol: Paul Toothill

Leeth: Michael Mayard
Searchers: Derek Broome,
  David Cann
Pilot: Michael Spice
Controller: Hugh Dickson

# SERIES C

Series Script Editor: Chris Boucher
Series Producer: David Maloney

## 1. AFTERMATH, transmitted Monday 7th January 1980

Author: Terry Nation
Director: Vere Lorrimer

Hal Mellanby: Cy Grant
Chel: Alan Lake
Lauren: Sally Harrison

First Trooper: Richard Franklin
Second Trooper: Michael Melia

## 2. POWERPLAY, transmitted Monday 14th January 1980

Author: Terry Nation
Director: David Maloney

Klegg: Michael Sheard
Harmon: Doyne Byrd
Lom: John Hollis
Mall: Michael Crane

Zee: Primi Townsend
Barr: Julia Vidler
Nurse: Catherine Chase
Receptionist: Helen Batch

## 3. VOLCANO, transmitted Monday 21st January 1980

Author: Allan Prior
Director: Desmond McCarthy

Hower: Michael Gough
Bershar: Malcom Bullivant
Mori: Ben Howard
Mutoid: Judy Matheson

Battle Fleet Commander: Alan Bowerman
Robot: Guy Hassan
Milus: Russell Denton

## 4. DAWN OF THE GODS, transmitted Monday 28th January 1980

Author: James Follett
Director: Desmond McCarthy

The Caliph: Sam Dastor          Groff: Terry Scully
The Thaarn: Marcus Powell

## 5. THE HARVEST OF KAIROS, transmitted Monday 4th February 1980

Author: Ben Steed
Director: Gerald Blake

Jarvik: Andrew Burt
Dastor: Frank Gatliff
Shad: Anthony Gardner
Guard: Charles Jamieson
Carlon: Sam Davies
Labourer: Stuart Fell

First and Third Leader:
    Christopher Douglas
Interceptor Captain and
    Leader Two: Hywel
    David

## 6. THE CITY AT THE EDGE OF THE WORLD, transmitted Monday 11th February 1980

Author: Chris Boucher
Director: Vere Lorrimer

Kerril: Carol Hawkins          Sherm: John J. Carney
Bayban: Colin Baker            Norl: Valentine Dyall

## 7. CHILDREN OF AURON, transmitted Tuesday 19th February 1980

Author: Roger Parkes
Director: Andrew Morgan

Deral: Rio Fanning
Ginka: Ric Young
Patar: Jack McKenzie
CA Two: Beth Harris

CA One: Ronald Leigh-Hunt
Franton: Sarah Atkinson
Pilot Four-Zero: Michael
    Troughton

19

## 8. RUMOURS OF DEATH, transmitted Monday 25th February 1980

Author: Chris Boucher
Director: Fiona Cumming

| | |
|---|---|
| Shrinker: John Bryans | Grenlee: Donald Douglas |
| Chesku: Peter Clay | Forres: David Haig |
| Sula: Lorna Heilbron | Balon: Philip Bloomfield |
| | Hob: David Gillies |

## 9. SARCOPHAGUS, transmitted Monday 3rd March 1980

Author: Tanith Lee
Director: Fiona Cumming

## 10. ULTRAWORLD, transmitted Monday 10th March 1980

Author: Trevor Hoyle
Director: Vere Lorrimer

| | |
|---|---|
| Ultra One: Peter Irchards | Ultra Three: Ian Barritt |
| Ultra Two: Stephen Jenn | Relf: Ronald Govey |

## 11. MOLOCH, transmitted Monday 17th March 1980

Author: Ben Steed
Director: Vere Lorrimer

| | |
|---|---|
| Grose: John Hartley | Chesil: Sabina Franklyn |
| Lector: Mark Sheridan | Poola: Debbi Blythe |
| Doran: Davyd Harries | Moloch: Deep Roy |

## 12. DEATH-WATCH, transmitted Monday 24th March 1980

Author: Chris Boucher
Director: Gerald Blake

| | |
|---|---|
| Karla: Kathy Iddon | Max: Stewart Bevan |
| Commentator: David Sibley | Vinni: Mark Elliott |

13. **TERMINAL,** transmitted Monday 31st March 1980

Author: Terry Nation
Director: Mary Ridge

Kostos: Gillian McCutcheon    Toron: Richard Clifford
Reeval: Heather Wright    Sphere Voice: David Healy

# SERIES D

Series Script Editor: Chris Boucher
Series Producer: Vere Lorrimer

1. **RESCUE,** transmitted Monday 28th September 1981

Author: Chris Boucher
Director: Mary Ridge

Dorian: Geoffrey Burridge    The Creature: Rob Middleton

2. **POWER,** transmitted Monday 5th October 1981

Author: Ben Steed
Director: Mary Ridge

Gun-Sar: Dicken Ashworth    Niria: Jenny Oulton
Kate: Alison Glennie    Cato: Paul Ridley
Luxia: Linda Barr

3. **TRAITOR,** transmitted Monday 12th October 1981

Author: Robert Holmes
Director: David Sullivan Proudfoot

Leitz: Malcolm Stoddard    Forbus: Edgar Wreford
Colonel Quute: Christopher    General: Nick Brimble
  Neame    The Tracer: David Quilter
Major Hunda: Robert Morris    Avandir: Neil Dickson
Practor: John Quentin

## 4. STARDRIVE, transmitted Monday 19th October 1981
Author: Jim Follett
Director: David Sullivan Proudfoot

Dr Plaxton: Barbara Shelley
Atlan: Damien Thomas
Bomber: Peter Sands
Napier: Leonard Kavanagh

## 5. ANIMALS, transmitted Monday 26th October 1981
Author: Allan Prior
Director: Mary Ridge

Justin: Peter Byrne
Captain: William Lindsay
Borr: Max Harvey
Ardus: Kevin Stoney
Og: David Boyce

## 6. HEADHUNTER, transmitted Monday 2nd November 1981
Author: Roger Parkes
Director: Mary Ridge

Muller: John Westbrook
Vena: Lynda Bellingham
Technician: Douglas Fielding
Android: Nick Joseph
Voice: Lesley Nunnerley

## 7. ASSASSIN, transmitted Monday 9th November 1981
Author: Rod Beacham
Director: David Sullivan Proudfoot

Verlis: Betty Marsden
Nebrox: Richard Hurndall
Piri: Caroline Holdaway
Cancer: John Wyman
Benos: Peter Attad
Tok: Adam Blackwood
Servant's Captain: Mark
Barratt

## 8. GAMES, transmitted Monday 16th November 1981
Author: Bill Lyons
Director: Vivienne Cozens

Belkov: Stratford Johns
Gambit: Rosalind Bailey
Gerren: David Neal
Computer: Michael Gaunt
Guard: James Harvey

### 9. SAND, transmitted Monday 23rd November 1981

Author: Tanith Lee
Director: Vivienne Cozens

Reeve: Stephen Yardley
Chasgow: Daniel Hill
Servalan's Assistant: Peter Craze

Keller: Jonathan David
Computer: Michael Gaunt

### 10. GOLD, transmitted Monday 30th November 1981

Author: Colin Davis
Director: Brian Lighthill

Keiller: Roy Kinnear
Doctor: Anthony Brown

Woman Passenger: Dinah May
Pilot: Norman Hartley

### 11. ORBIT, transmitted Monday 7th December 1981

Author: Robert Holmes
Director: Brian Lighthill

Egrorian: John Savident

Pinder: Larry Noble

### 12. WARLORD, transmitted Monday 14th December 1981

Author: Simon Masters
Director: Viktors Ritelis

Zukan: Roy Boyd
Zeeona: Bobbie Brown
Finn: Dean Harris

Boorva: Simon Merrick
Chalsa: Rick James
Lod: Charles Augins

Mida: Brian Spink

### 13. BLAKE, transmitted Monday 21st December 1981

Author: Chris Boucher
Director: Mary Ridge

Deva: David Collings
Klyn: Janet Lee Price

Arlen: Sasha Mitchell

# The Writers

## TERRY NATION – Series Creator

Terry started out as a comedian, but on being told that his jokes were all right but he wasn't funny, he turned to writing. Subsequently he wrote over 200 radio shows for leading comics followed by spectaculars and comedy series for television. He later turned to drama and produced a number of science fiction plays for television. He also wrote more episodes of 'The Saint' than any other writer, before being hired to write seven 'Dr Who' episodes (namely the series which introduced the Daleks). Since then he has been script supervisor and principal writer on 'The Avengers' and 'The Persuaders', produced a best selling children's book 'Rebecca's World', and written the book and television series 'Survivors'. Since 1979 Terry has worked as a writer/producer for Columbia Pictures and 20th Century Fox, and now lives permanently in Los Angeles.

## ROD BEACHAM

Born in 1940, Rod's early life was spent in England, Japan and South Africa. From 1961 to 1963 he studied at the Royal Academy of Dramatic Art and then became an actor with the National Theatre and various reps. Subsequently he has played Jack Munro in Waggoners Walk, and has performed in as many as three West End plays a week. However since his first radio play, 'Sunday Voice', he has turned almost completely to writing, with six more radio plays adding to earlier success as a TV playwright.

## CHRIS BOUCHER

Born in 1943, Chris travelled extensively before gaining a BA in economics from Essex University, where he began to write. After working in a variety of odd jobs he started writing for television, contributing to such series as 'Braden's Week', 'Saturday Crowd', 'Don't Ask Us We're New Here', 'Lulu', 'Dave Allen at Large', 'Romany Jones', 'That's Life' etc. He wrote three four-part stories for 'Dr Who' before becoming Script Editor of 'Blake's 7'. Since working on Blake he has been script editor for 'Juliet Bravo', has written the radio serial 'A Walk in the Dark', adapted Harry Harrison's 'The Technicolour Time Machine' for radio, and written episodes of 'Shoestring' and 'Bureau 286'.

## JAMES FOLLETT

James was born in 1939 and trained as a marine engineer. Following a career writing manuals for the Ministry of Defence he turned to radio, since which time innumerable radio scripts have been broadcast by the BBC, with perhaps the best known being the two ten-part series 'Earthsearch' and 'Earthsearch II'. For television he has written scripts for 'Crown Court' and 'The Squad', as well as for the BBC Schools series 'Today and Tomorrow'. He has written eight novels including the two 'Earthsearch' series, and has novelised the film 'Who Dares Wins'.

## ROBERT HOLMES

Robert has been writing for television since 1960, notably on such science qction series as Undermind n Doomwatch' and Dr Who m Episodes of shoestring'n Juliet Bravo and the BBC 1 serial The Nightmare Man are among his most recently transmitted work.

## TREVOR HOYLE

Trevor has had some twenty novels published in various genres including thrillers, mainstream, science fiction, documentary and spy, of which the most recent are 'Seeking the Mythical Future', 'Through the Eye of Time' and 'The Gods Look Down'. Other Trevor Hoyle titles include 'The Man Who Travelled Motorways', 'Bullet Train' and the three Blake novels – 'Blake's Seven', 'Blake's Seven and Project Avalon', and 'Blake's Seven Scorpio Attack'. He has written short stories for *Mayfair, Men Only, Transatlantic Review,* and Radio 4.

## TANITH LEE

Tanith is the author of four radio plays, two television scripts and about thirty novels, including some for children. Most of her books have only been published in the USA, but among those available in the UK are 'The Birthgrave Trilogy' (consisting of 'The Birthgrave', 1977, 'Shadowfire', 1978, and 'Quest for the White Witch', 1979, all published by Futura), 'The Storm Lord', Futura, 1977, 'Drinking Sapphire Wine/Don't Bite The Sun', Hamlyn, 1979, and 'Night's Master', Hamlyn, 1981.

## BILL LYONS

Bill has written for many popular series including 'Z Cars', 'Angels', 'Rooms', 'Marked Personal' and 'Juliet Bravo', as well as such long running soap operas as 'Crossroads' and 'Waggoners Walk'. In 1973 HRH Prince Phillip presented him with the Writers Guild Award for the 'Best British Dramatic Script in the Field of Education'. Amongst his many BBC plays are 'One Third of the Wise Men' about his father, the late Lord Lyons, public relations advisor to Sir Harold Wilson.

## SIMON MASTERS

Born in 1948, Simon began his career as a novelist with two books published whilst still in his teens. Before he was twenty-one he had produced a stage play, two film scripts and an official history of the National Youth Theatre, of which he was a member. He became a BBC Script Editor in 1971, working on 'Poldark', 'Horseman Riding By', 'Spy Trap' and several Francis Durbridge thrillers. Since leaving the BBC in 1978 he has written two more novels, a radio play, a film script and episodes for 'Onedin Line' and 'Juliet Bravo'.

## ROGER PARKES

Roger worked as a reporter and later foreign correspondent with Beaverbrook Newspapers, and as Editor of Farming Express, before becoming a story editor with the BBC, working on 'Out of the Unknown' and 'Make Mine Murder'. He has also written episodes for 'Six Days of Justice', 'The Prisoner', 'Harriet's Back in Town', 'Marked Personal', 'Warship', 'The Expert', 'Man in a

Suitcase', 'The Strange Report', 'Z Cars', 'Onedin Line', 'Crown Court', 'Goodbye Darling', 'Maybury', 'Angels', 'Survivors', and 'Doomwatch'. He has also had four thrillers and a novel 'The Fourth Monkey' published and is currently working on a play for the 'Jackanory Playhouse' series.

## ALAN PRIOR

Alan has written some twelve novels including 'One Away', which received the British Critics Award and an award for the best foreign novel in France. Another novel, 'The Interrogators', won the *Books and Bookman* Award for the best novel of the year. Alan has also written the scripts for film versions of these novels, and the film rights to another novel, 'The Operators', have been sold. His work on television includes scripts for 'Spy', 'Z Cars', 'Softly Softly', 'Task Force', 'Dr Who', 'Junior ward', 'Shoestring', 'The Onedin Line' and 'Secret Army', as well as a number of original TV plays for which he has won five awards.

## BEN STEED

Ben has had over 200 short stories published, and his episodes for television series include work on 'Coronation Street', 'Crown Court', 'Buccaneer', 'For Maddie with Love', 'Masterspy', 'Starting Out', 'Jackanory Playhouse' and 'Triangle'. He has also written an adaptation of Jerome K Jerome's 'Malvinia of Brittany'. In addition he has written three radio plays.

# The Stories

## SERIES A EPISODE 1
## THE WAY BACK

Roj Blake meets two colleagues who persuade him to go illegally outside the dome in which they live on Earth. The aim is for Blake to meet former colleagues of whom, strangely, he has no memory. Blake's friends inform him that he was once a major resistance leader but after capture had his mind re-programmed so that he would renounce his old colleagues and give evidence against them.

Blake goes outside and attends a rebels' meeting, but hides when guards appear and kill everyone present. Blake escapes only to be recaptured upon re-entering the city, where he is put on trial for a series of crimes against children. Despite the fact that the evidence is completely fabricated, he is found guilty and sentenced to transportation to the planet Cygnus Alpha. Blake's defence attorney becomes uneasy about certain aspects of the trial and starts to investigate on his own. He gradually comes up with evidence to prove not only Blake's innocence but also the complete fabrication of the evidence against him by senior Administration officials, which he takes before a superior, who turns out to be fully implicated in the invention of the evidence against Blake. Whilst continuing to try to gather information to clear Blake, the attorney is murdered by Federation guards.

Whilst Blake is waiting to board the space ship to

Cygnus Alpha, he meets Jenna and Vila for the first time. Blake is still hoping for a reprieve when time runs out and the ship takes off. As the ship leaves Earth, Blake vows to return one day.

## SERIES A EPISODE 2
## SPACE FALL

Blake and the others are on the space ship London en route for Cygnus Alpha. Blake organises a rebellion with the help of some of his fellow convicts. Avon breaks through to the computer room and temporarily puts the computer out of action whilst Blake and the others break free from their quarters. However, due to Vila's inability to follow Gan's straightforward orders, the rebellion is quashed.

Blake, Jenna and Avon barricade themselves temporarily in the computer room, but finally give themselves up when Raiker, one of the ship's officers, starts killing other prisoners.

Meanwhile, the ship London has been buffeted by very severe shock waves from what is presumed to be a space battle between two alien fleets. Eventually, one of the ships from the battle drifts unpowered and unmanned alongside the London and Leylan, the London's commander, sends three of his crew across to investigate it: two of these die and one goes mad. Raiker then persuades his captain to send Blake, Avon and Jenna across. They experience the Liberator's defence mechanism, which implants in their minds images from their past in order to disorientate and kill them. Blake, however, is able to resist, possibly through his recollection of having been interfered with mentally by the Federation. He destroys the defence mechanism and the three close the outer hatch, thus stopping anyone else from boarding the ship. Jenna then manages to get the Liberator underway.

# SERIES A EPISODE 3
## CYGNUS ALPHA

Blake, Avon and Jenna explore the space ship Liberator which they have just taken over and establish contact with the master computer Zen, enabling them to fly the ship. They also discover the teleport system, which Blake uses for the first time when the ship arrives at Cygnus Alpha. A further discovery is a set of hand guns of immense power.

Meanwhile the space transporter London has unloaded its passengers and lifted off again to return to Earth. The prisoners arriving on the planet are greeted by the priests and priestesses who rule Cygnus Alpha. Blake uses the teleport system for the second time in order to find the prisoners and rescue them. He leaves instructions that he is to be recalled within four hours.

Blake discovers that the prisoners are suffering from a sickness which infects everyone who is on Cygnus Alpha for more than an hour, and he is told that there is no cure for the sickness apart from regular doses of a serum available only on the planet. Meanwhile back on the Liberator, Avon and Jenna discover rooms full of clothes and immense hoards of precious jewels.

Blake's attempt to release the prisoners fails and he is captured. Vargas, the ruler of the planet, demands that Blake hand over his ship so that he, Vargas, can travel through the galaxy, spreading his religion.

On the Liberator, Avon is trying to convince Jenna of the pointlessness of waiting for Blake. However, Jenna persuades him to wait, and with just a few minutes of the four hours remaining, Blake calls in for teleportation. After further argument, Jenna teleports Blake, Gan and Vila up. However, she also unwittingly teleports Vargas, who reveals that the sickness from which everyone has been suffering is merely a passing thing and that no antidote is required at all. Blake teleports him into space, where he dies immediately. Zen then reports that some

31

Federation Pursuit Ships are homing in on the Liberator, and Blake and the new crew begin their escape flight.

# SERIES A EPISODE 4
# TIME SQUAD

Blake is determined to attack the Federation and thus change the status of his crew from minor irritants into a major problem. He decides to strike at the communications complex on the planet Saurian Major. Whilst en route for the planet the crew of the Liberator answer an emergency signal and take on board a small projectile which appears to contain three aliens in cryogenic suspension. One of the aliens has died through a malfunction of his chamber, but two remain and the Liberator's crew take steps to revive them. Blake, Vila and Avon teleport to Saurian Major in order to locate the resistance forces on the planet, with whom they hope to launch a strong attack on the Federation complex.

Once on the planet, they are attacked by Cally, a native of the planet Auron who has telepathic ability. She reveals that she is the only survivor of a guerilla force that was attacking the Federation. She joins Blake and the others and they break into the communications complex.

Meanwhile, on the Liberator, Jenna and Gan are keeping watch on the ship and on the aliens. Gan explains to Jenna that he is unable to kill because of the Limiter placed in his head by the Federation after he had killed a Federation guard. Gan goes to check on the aliens and discovers that the two have already left the capsule. They overpower him, and his Limiter prevents him from killing them. Zen identifies the aliens as guardians of a set of genetic banks carried in their projectile. The guardians and gene bank together represent a complete invasion force, and the guardians will attack anyone and everyone who is seen as a threat to their genetic banks.

Whilst Jenna and Gan are struggling with the aliens, Blake and the rest of the crew, with Cally, set explosive devices within the computer complex. But when Blake tries to get the Liberator to teleport them back there is no response, for at that moment Jenna comes under attack from a previously unsuspected fourth alien and Gan, still suffering from his previous experience, is unable to help her.

Eventually, Gan manages to teleport the four back to the Liberator and to overpower the fourth alien. Cally then agrees to join the Liberator, thus making six crew members, with Zen bringing it up to seven.

## SERIES A EPISODE 5
## THE WEB

After a very short time on board the Liberator, Cally has already attempted to sabotage the ship. However her sabotage attempt appears to have brought severe injury upon herself, and although she does not give any outward signs the crew conclude that she must be suffering intense pain. The sabotaged Liberator rushes out of control through space until it is trapped in a web surrounding an unknown, unnamed planet. The crew make several unsuccessful attempts to free the Liberator from the web until the drain on the energy banks becomes too great to permit escape.

Jenna begins to speak in a strange voice and relays to Blake an instruction to land the ship. Instead he teleports down to the planet alone.

Blake meets what appear to be the survivors of a centuries-old experimental project in the forbidden field of genetic engineering. The experiment was run by outlawed members of Cally's people, the Auronas, who have used their telepathic powers to communicate with her and thus force her to bring the ship to their planet.

They have created two types of beings, one humanoid and apparently intelligent, the other, the Decimas, a race of machine-animals created to undertake basic menial tasks. However the Decimas appear to have got out of control: they are able to breed and are now breeding in emotions and violent habits which were never programmed into them originally.

The two genetically engineered people on the planet are under the control of a withered humanoid suspended in liquid who seems to contain the memories of the six original members of the experimental expedition. He wishes to have his energy banks replaced, after which he promises to clear a way through the web. But he also reveals that he plans to use the energy to wipe out the Decimas. Blake objects to this on moral grounds.

Avon teleports down with the energy reserves and Blake realises that he has teleported to an area thick with Decimas. Fearing for his safety and rather than teleporting him back to the ship, Blake takes the two humanoids out with him to search for Avon.

Whilst the research project remains unguarded, the Decimas begin an attack. Blake attempts to negotiate with the humanoids but without success. They are marched back to the dome and the new power sources put in place, but the Decimas' attack overpowers the Auronar. Blake and Avon use the power source to destroy the web and the Liberator escapes just ahead of a group of Federation Pursuit Ships.

## SERIES A EPISODE 6
## SEEK-LOCATE-DESTROY

Blake decides to launch a raid which will enable him to steal a message decoder from a top security installation on Centero. The plan involves blowing up part of the installation so that the Federation will not realise immediately that that particular device has been stolen and thus will not be tempted to change their coding system. All of the crew except Jenna teleport down, set the charges and remove the decoding device.

However Cally, who is holding a group of prisoners whilst the others continue with their work, is attacked when she takes her eyes off the prisoners for a moment. She loses her teleportation bracelet in the ensuing scuffle and is still searching for it when the explosions go off. The rest of the crew do not realise that she is missing for some time, and by then the Liberator is many spacials distant and being pursued by missiles launched from Centero.

Meanwhile on the station, which serves as Space Command headquarters, Supreme Commander Servalan is being questioned by two representatives of the President. They express the President's dismay that Blake is not only still alive but is becoming a hero of malcontents and opponents to the Federation. Despite major opposition from these two envoys, she appoints Space Commander Travis to lead the hunt for Blake.

Back on Centero, Cally survives the explosions and is taken prisoner.

Travis realises that the explosions were merely to mislead him and recognises that the decoding device has been stolen. He persuades Servalan not to change the codes immediately, but to take advantage of the position to broadcast a message which Blake is bound to pick up and respond to. The message chosen states that Cally has been found alive. Blake immediately takes the ship back to Centero and, despite his knowledge that there will be large numbers of forces out to stop him, produces a plan which involves taking the Liberator into very close range, teleporting him to the interrogation room where Cally is being held, and releasing her. He does this to avoid Travis's knowing exactly when the ship is going to teleport him down. He succeeds in releasing Cally and they teleport back to the ship. Travis vows vengeance,

Ships crewed by mutoids, he commences the long chase which is only concluded at the outbreak of the Intergalactic War.

## SERIES A EPISODE 7
## MISSION TO DESTINY

The Liberator encounters a Galaxy Class cruiser, Ortega, circling helplessly in space. Blake, Avon and Cally teleport across and find that the pilot of the ship has been murdered and the rest of the crew rendered unconscious by gas rigged up to the air supply. The controls have been severely damaged so as to keep the ship in a circling orbit. However there is no indication of who was responsible or why. The Liberator crew stop the tranquilising gas from circulating and recycle normal air. They then talk with the crew of the ship and discover that it is taking a neutrotope back to its home planet, Destiny, where it will be put in orbit in order to neutralise some of the rays of the star around which Destiny moves. In this way a deadly fungus which is killing the plant life on the planet will be destroyed and Destiny's agricultural economy will be able to continue as before.

Blake offers to take the neutrotope to Destiny on the Liberator whilst Cally and Avon remain on the Ortega in order to effect repairs. Although Kendall, the leader of Ortega's crew agrees at once, some of the rest of the crew are uneasy about the situation; however a majority of one allows Blake to take the neutrotope onto the Liberator.

On the way to Destiny, the Liberator comes into contact with a huge meteorite storm which seriously drains the energy banks. During the storm the container holding the neutrotope moves from its position on the table and drops onto the floor. Checking for damage, Blake finds that they have been given an empty container and that the neutrotope is still clearly on board the

Ortega, towards which he immediately turns the Liberator.

On board Ortega, meanwhile, a second body has been discovered, and soon after there is a third murder. However the murderer and reason for murdering are still unknown, although it is suggested that anyone who got hold of the neutrotope would be in an ideal bargaining position, holding as they would the future of an entire planet in their hands. It then becomes evident that there is a space ship approaching the Ortega, presumably to rendezvous with the murderer and possessor of the neutrotope.

Avon realises that a message left by the murdered pilot in his own blood was in fact not coded, but merely the result of the pilot's hand faltering as he died. He then translates the murderer's name as that of the girl Sara, who immediately admits responsibility and locks herself into the pilot's cabin to await the ship that will take her and the neutrotope away.

Avon arranges a masquerade to make it sound as if the rescue ship has landed and a fight is going on outside. This induces Sara to come out of the cabin and she is immediately grabbed and put under arrest. The entire crew of the Ortega teleport back to the Liberator in order to be taken to their planet Destiny. At the last moment Sara throws away her bracelet and thus avoids teleportation. However the moment the rescue ship docks with the Ortega there is a massive explosion, Blake having rigged up explosive devices on the docking mechanism, and Sara is killed.

# SERIES A EPISODE 8
# DUEL

The Liberator has used up a lot of its energy supplies in trying to evade the Pursuit Ships. They approach a completely uncharted planet and take a very low orbit in order to spend forty-eight hours recharging the energy banks. Whilst this is happening, Blake, Jenna and Gan teleport down to the surface, where they find millions upon millions of graves and the signs of a series of battles having taken place many years before. They also spot two aliens who appear and then disappear.

Meanwhile Travis, with two Pursuit Ships, approaches the Liberator. Blake and the others rapidly teleport back to the ship and attempt to engage in battle. However, with their energy reserves so low, they find it exceptionally difficult. They ride out a number of plasma bolt attacks until Blake hits on the idea of ramming Travis's ship. As the two ships are about to connect, all motion is stopped and Sinofar and Giroc, the two aliens, take control from the surface, bringing Blake and Travis down to the planet.

It appears that they are the last survivors of an ancient race which destroyed itself in wars thousands of years before. Between them they control the Power, all that remains of that race. They announce that Blake and Travis must fight a duel in order to learn the lessons of their race. Each man is given a knife and told that he must hunt the other. A friend of each is also teleported down to the surface, in Blake's case Jenna and in Travis's the mutoid pilot of his ship. They are transported to a forest and the hunt begins as night falls.

Travis and his mutoid set a trap for Blake whilst Blake and Jenna remain in a tree, avoiding the probably violent animals which still range over the planet's surface. The mutoid captures Jenna, and in her desperate need is about to take Jenna's blood, when Travis intervenes and tells her to leave Jenna as a trap. Blake finds Jenna and starts to release her as Travis springs his trap. Blake wins the ensuing fight and Jenna overpowers the mutoid, who is weak with lack of blood.

Despite having won the battle, Blake refuses to kill Travis in order to teach Sinofar and Giroc a lesson about mercy. They allow Blake to return to the Liberator and recharge the energy banks for the crew, thus allowing them to escape before Travis and the now disgraced mutoid can return to their ship.

# SERIES A EPISODE 9
# PROJECT AVALON

In an attempt to rescue Avalon, a resistance leader, Blake and the Liberator travel to an icy planet where Avalon has been leading a resistance movement. Upon arriving, they discover that many people lie dead around the site chosen for the rendezvous and Avalon is missing. In fact, Avalon has been captured by Travis, who is working on a plan to kill the crew of the Liberator whilst leaving the Liberator undamaged. Chevner, one of Avalon's assistants, has survived and helps Blake, Jenna and Vila work their way through tunnels towards the command centre where Avalon is being held.

Despite being totally outnumbered and, surprisingly, hit by bullets from Federation weapons, Blake and the others successfully capture Avalon and teleport back to the Liberator. It is then that Blake realises something is seriously wrong. His suspicions fall initially on the assistant Chevner, but when he is found dead it becomes apparent that the Avalon on board is in reality an android. She is carrying a small sphere which when crushed will release a deadly plague that will kill the crew of the Liberator and liquidate itself within minutes, leaving the ship uncontaminated.

The Liberator is returned to its previous position whilst Avon reprogrammes the android. Blake teleports back down with the android, who still holds the plague sphere. He negotiates the release of Avalon and leaves the android on the surface holding the sphere. Despite the fact that he saves all present, including Servalan, from the fatal plague by catching the sphere as it falls from the android's hand, Travis is relieved by Servalan of all his duties because of the failure of Project Avalon.

## SERIES A EPISODE 10
## BREAKDOWN

During a series of standard manoeuvres, the limiter placed in Gan's brain begins to malfunction and he becomes unusually aggressive, assaulting members of the crew and using his enormous strength to attack the Liberator itself. He is eventually overpowered by the others, who then try to determine how and where they can obtain the skilled surgery required to repair the damage to Gan's limiter. Eventually, after much discussion, they decide to go to the space research station XK72, a location which Avon has already investigated as a possible place to go should he no longer be able to stay with Blake and the others on the Liberator.

The station houses a famous neurosurgeon, Professor Kayn, and it is to him they hope to turn. However, in order to get to XK72 in time, it is necessary to travel through an exceptionally dangerous zone of space. Zen refuses to fly the ship through this zone, and when the ship is taken through on manual control, Zen disengages all functions. This means that the ship gradually becomes more and more unstable, since the computers are a central part of the Liberator's design system. Avon just manages to bypass Zen as they are about to be drawn into the very centre of a gravitational vortex. With the computers back on line, they fly through the centre of the vortex and reach XK72.

Recognising that the doctors on XK72 are unlikely to help Blake if they realise that the Liberator is a ship full of criminals, they pretend to be a Federation ship on a practice run. Professor Kayn, however, quickly divines what is going on. Despite being on a neutral space station, his sympathies towards law and order lead him to alert the Federation to Blake's whereabouts and three Pursuit Ships are rapidly sent. With only thirty minutes to go he begins the operation on Liberator, warning the crew that Gan will die if they attempt to move out of the range of the space station, since any vibration will affect the outcome of the operation. The operation is successfully completed with minutes to spare, and Kayn and his assistant are transported back to XK72 as the Liberator turns to make its escape.

A furious argument breaks out on XK72 concerning the legitimacy of Kayn's notification of the Federation forces, and during the dispute Kayn strangles the station administrator, Farren. He then becomes so distraught at the destruction wrought by his own hands, hands normally used to save life, that he sits helpless as a Federation plasma bolt deflected off the Liberator's screens approaches and destroys XK72.

## SERIES A EPISODE 11
## BOUNTY

The Federation have been interfering in the affairs of the planet Lindor and have fixed an election in order to ensure the defeat of President Sarkoff. The President has been taken to an unnamed planet and held under a loose form of arrest whilst the Federation develops its grip on Lindor. In order to prevent the planet from falling completely into Federation hands, Blake and Cally teleport down to where Sarkoff is being held in the hopes of convincing him of the need to travel back to Lindor and take command once more. Whilst Blake and Cally are working their way into the ancient house in which the ex-President is held, the Liberator picks up a distress call and goes after the ship that is emitting it.

On Lindor Blake and Cally find Sarkoff and his

daughter Tyce surrounded by a collection of 20th-century Earth artifacts. Along with Tyce, these are apparently all that he now values, and he has little desire to return to his planet, harbouring bitter feelings that his people have rejected him. Tyce however is tired of her father's inactivity and seeks to help Blake and Cally in their plan to re-inspire him.

Back on the Liberator, Gan has teleported across to the ship from which the distress call was emanating, only to find that a trap has been set by a group of Amagons who wish to capture the Liberator and its crew and sell it to the Federation at a tremendous profit. The Amagons capture the crew, and when Blake, Cally, Sarkoff and Tyce teleport back they too are captured. It appears initially that Jenna has made a deal with the Amagon leader, Tarvin, whom she had known during her smuggling days. However, she double-crosses Tarvin and knocks out two of the guards before Avon breaks free from the room in which the crew are being held. The Amagons are then overpowered. Sarkoff finally gives in to Tyce's request that he be transported back to Lindor and once more take up government of the planet.


# SERIES A EPISODE 12
# DELIVERANCE

The crew of the Liberator witness the explosion and crash of a space craft as it approaches the planet Cephlon. Avon, Vila, Jenna and Gan decide to teleport down to look for survivors from the capsules that were ejected as the space craft exploded, although they are aware of the high radioactivity on the surface which means that they will be unable to stay very long. One of the two crew members is dead – the other is badly injured and is brought back to the Liberator. During this time, Jenna is captured and taken prisoner by a group of primitives.

Back at Space Command headquarters, Servalan receives a report of the crash and explains to Travis what has led up to the event. Ensor, a scientist living in isolation with his son on the planet Aristo, had developed the greatest computer ever known. He was in need of medical attention, and his son had travelled to Federation headquarters in order to bargain. He had arranged for Servalan to buy Orac, the computer, for 100 million credits on the understanding that she would also send a surgeon to Aristo to restore the elder Ensor to health. However, not having the authority to deliver such vast sums of money, Servalan has double-crossed the younger Ensor by placing a bomb on board his ship. It was this that caused the explosion near the planet Cephlon which the Liberator's crew happened to see. Hearing that the explosion has now occurred, Servalan makes ready to leave for Aristo with Travis.

Meanwhile, on the planet's surface Avon, Vila and Gan are searching for Jenna and come across the remains of an abandoned civilisation guarded by a priestess. Avon speaks to her first and she imagines that he must be a lord sent from the gods as promised in the prophecies of her people. Avon, Vila and Gan soon understand that the priestess is in fact guarding an ancient space ship headquarters which remains fully intact and operational and where, just outside, a space ship stands ready for launch. The ship carries millions of cells representing the race which had originally inhabited Cephlon but was mostly wiped out in a series of wars, which also explains the high level of radiation on the planet.

Back on the Liberator, the young Ensor has recovered sufficiently to come to the flight deck, where he takes Cally hostage and demands to be taken to Aristo at once. However he has been so badly injured that after several hours he collapses and dies, leaving Blake free to turn the Liberator round and take it back to Cephlon. There Avon, Vila and Gan rescue Jenna from the savages and launch the rocket which the priestess Meegat had been guarding, after which they return to the Liberator. By this time, Blake has become intrigued about the mysterious Orac of which he has no details and has agreed with the dying Ensor to take the needed power units to his father on Aristo.

## SERIES A  EPISODE 13
## ORAC

Following their encounter with the young Ensor, the crew of the Liberator decide to travel to Aristo in order to deliver the life-saving supplies to his father and also find out the true nature of Orac. Meanwhile, unknown to Blake, Travis and Servalan are making a similar journey. Whilst en route for Aristo, the members of the Liberator crew who have been on Cephlon begin to show all the signs of advanced radiation sickness. It is then discovered that there are no anti-radiation drugs on board, so the journey to Aristo is speeded up in hopes that Ensor will be able to provide them.

Upon reaching the planet, Blake and Cally, the only two not suffering from radiation sickness, teleport down – although the ship's computers have been interfered with and a precise fix for the teleport system has been manipulated from the planet. They arrive on a sea shore and, following instructions from a strange flying computer, are led to the underground city in which the elder Ensor is dying.

Travis and Servalan, having been unable to penetrate the force field surrounding Ensor, decide to try going under it by using old tunnels beneath the city. These are now inhabited by strange reptilian creatures which delay but do not totally stop their progress.

Blake and Cally convince Ensor that his one chance of survival is to teleport back to the ship with them, where the operation he needs can be performed. But they are

44

unable to teleport through the force field generated from Ensor's room and they too must make their way back to the shore. Just then Travis and Servalan break through a wall and, seeing Blake head for the underground route out of the base, take an alternative route which gets them to the surface before him.

Ensor suffers a final heart attack on the way and so dies, but not before he can pass the computer Orac over to Blake. On the surface, Blake and Cally are ambushed by Servalan and Travis, but before they can be killed and Orac stolen, Vila and Avon come to their rescue.

On the Liberator, the members of the crew suffering from radiation sickness receive the necessary course of radiation drugs and all gather round to investigate Orac's powers. It reveals itself to have the voice and personality of Ensor, and to require very specific requests for information, without which it refuses to act. Blake orders Orac to make one prediction, and in fulfilment of this order Orac projects a picture of the Liberator onto the ship's main screen. This image is then seen to explode. Although the crew then turn Orac off, they recognise that the prediction has already been made and presumably will come to pass, and they are left wondering what to do about it.

# SERIES B EPISODE 1
## REDEMPTION

Avon tells Blake that one way to defy Orac's prediction concerning the destruction of the Liberator would be to examine the position of the stars shown behind the ship in Orac's projection and then avoid travelling there. This is done, and the star positions indicate a sector of the galaxy far removed from the Liberator's present position – the crew therefore agree to make sure the Liberator stays well outside that sector.

Suddenly the Liberator comes under attack from two non-Federation space ships showing great speed and technical fighting ability. Instead of destroying the Liberator, however, the alien ships knock out Liberator's weapon system and take over the computer circuits. This leaves the Liberator travelling at full speed, but blind. The alien ships then withdraw and the crew of the Liberator attempt to effect repairs. They discover that, as they try to regain control, the ship rejects them. This culminates with various cables detaching themselves from their normal positions and attacking first Blake and then Avon in order to stop them from switching on the main drive unit.

It becomes clear from these events that the original designers and owners of the Liberator are taking their own property back. They do indeed board and take off various members of the crew before docking. It appears that they work for a massive computer complex in space known as the System. This complex services three planets which were formerly at war until one of the three developed the super-computer which took over the weaponry computers of the others. Although giving the three planets freedom from war and famine, the System has reduced much of the populace to slavery.

During the interrogation of Blake which follows, it becomes clear that the System is itself having computer problems and Blake concludes this must be the work of

Orac, which has up to this point refused all help, stating that it is already overloaded with analyses. Just before they are about to be killed, the crew manage to escape back to the Liberator and take it once more into space. However they immediately come under attack from an identical sister ship which launches plasma bolts against them. As they wait for their destruction, it is the sister ship instead of Liberator that blows up. Orac then explains that it had scrambled the weaponry system of the sister ship in order to make the original prediction of the destruction of a Liberator-like ship come true.

## SERIES B EPISODE 2
## SHADOW

Blake devises a plan to enlist the help of the Terra Nostra, an underground organisation dealing in, amongst other things, the drug Shadow. Blake aims to get the Terra Nostra to support the attempts of the Liberator's crew to undermine the Federation.

The Liberator travels to the entertainment satellite, Space City, where three of the crew negotiate with Largo, a leading Terra Nostran. At first Largo maintains that he has no contact with the Terra Nostra, but when the crew try to leave he imprisons them.

Hanna, an addict of Shadow, and her companion Bek, attempt to steal supplies of the drug from Largo. They find themselves imprisoned with Gan and Avon. Cally, realising the situation, threatens to destroy parts of Space City if the imprisoned crew members are not released. With the help of Bek and Hanna, Gan and Avon escape and release Blake and Jenna. All six return to the Liberator.

In the meantime, Vila has contravened direct orders from Blake and left the Liberator to visit Space City, having persuaded Orac to operate the teleport for him. In return Vila has acceded to Orac's unlikely request to be hidden within the Liberator so that it can get on with a project of its own.

Upon returning to the Liberator, Blake and the crew discover the origin of the drug Shadow and set course. En route, Cally happens upon the whereabouts of Orac and collapses under its influence. When she recovers she teleports to the planet surface, where she once more collapses. The Moon Discs which are the source of Shadow eventually come to Cally's rescue and she recovers consciousness. At the same time, the Liberator loses power dramatically and it is found that the power is being drained through Orac, now under alien control. Hanna tries to disconnect Orac and is killed in the process. Cally, in alliance with the Moon Discs, fights the aliens.

Whilst setting Explosive devices around the Moon Discs, Blake and the others meet Federation guards and come to the realisation that the Federation runs both the Moon Disc operation and the Terra Nostra. The devices are discharged, effectively wiping out the Moon Discs. Avon sets small charges within Orac, so that should it be tampered with again by an alien telepathic force, the charges will go off at once before any worse damage can be done.


# SERIES B EPISODE 3
# WEAPON

Coser, a Beta-class technician, has succeeded in developing a new weapon – Imipak. When his role in its development is ignored, Coser steals his own invention and, with the slave girl Rashel whom he has liberated, makes for a deserted planet. Upon arriving he destroys his own ship and camps out in the ruins of an old settlement.

Elsewhere, Servalan is planning to use Coser to

capture Blake. She makes a deal with the highly independent Clonemasters, who operate a cloning cartel. At least two clone Blakes are developed – the first is destroyed by Travis when he mistakes it for the real thing, and the second is taken to the planet on which Coser is hiding.

Servalan is aided in this venture by Carnell, a psycho-strategist who is able to make accurate predictions of the neurotic behaviour of Coser. Carnell suggests that Coser will be in such a terrible state from loneliness that he will be overjoyed to see the unreal Blake and will hand Imipak over willingly. Carnell ventures further that when a second Blake appears, Coser will go mad.

Blake, having heard of the security alert on the weapons development base, follows up the theft of Imipak by heading for the planet where Coser is hiding. Coser has already handed Imipak over to the clone Blake, and Travis uses it to shoot Blake and the Liberator crew. However, there will be no effect until the key trigger mechanism is pressed – something that can be delayed for years if need be.

Servalan lets the crew of Liberator escape, knowing that the Imipak key can not only be triggered over great time spans but also over great distances. She also knows that Travis·has been shot by the weapon and that when the key is used he too will die. However before any action can be taken Servalan and Travis are forced to hand the weapon over to the clone Blake and Rashel, who vow never to depress the key and set about building a home on their new planet. Sarvalan and Travis escape but Carnell, realising he has failed, leaves Servalan a message before deserting the Federation.

# SERIES B  EPISODE 4
# HORIZON

The crew of the Liberator are suffering nervous exhaustion following their series of close encounters with the Federation. They therefore take the Liberator into a distant part of the galaxy only to find, much to their surprise, a Federation Space Freighter passing nearby.

Out of curiosity, Blake follows the freighter to the planet Horizon, about which Zen has virtually no information. On finding that the freighter arrives only once a year, Blake's interest is further increased, and he and Jenna teleport down. They are quickly captured by a combination of Federation guards and natives using blow-pipes. Vila, Gan and Cally are likewise captured when they follow.

The captured crew members are put to work in the local mines, where a highly radioactive mineral is being dug by hand, though Blake first has a brief chance to talk to Ro, the native chief who has been made puppet ruler of the planet by the Federation. Ro is deeply influenced by his former tutor, now the local Federation Kommissar. Although Ro is clearly disturbed by some of Blake's revelations, he refuses to believe them until Cally produces facts suggesting that the Kommissar was involved in the death of Ro's own father.

Meanwhile, on the Liberator, Avon discusses with Orac the possibility of his survival if, as he assumes, none of the other members of the crew return. Orac confirms that it would be quite possible for Avon to survive to the natural end of his life providing he avoids a situation in which three Federation Pursuit Ships attack simultaneously. Whilst still considering this point, Avon is informed by Zen that there are at this moment three Federation Pursuit Ships homing in on Horizon, summoned by the Kommissar, who is concerned about Ro's reliability as a Federation puppet.

Having gathered information from Orac on the way in which the rest of the crew have probably been captured, Avon teleports to the surface and swiftly destroys the spying devices which have been disguised in the foliage. He kills several Federation guards and releases the crew,

50

who rapidly teleport back to the Ship. Blake then teleports back down to Ro's palace at the moment when Ro has abandoned his Federation uniform and returned to ceremonial tribal robes and blow-pipe. Blake kills the Assistant Kommissar, whilst Ro kills the Kommissar with a poisoned dart.

Back once more on the Liberator, Blake decides to leave the ship positioned directly in the course of the three Pursuit Ships, which unwittingly pass through Horizon's defence barrier and thus destroy themselves. Ro is left on the planet to free his people from the tyranny of Federation rule.


## SERIES B EPISODE 5
## PRESSURE POINT

The Liberator has returned to the vicinity of the Solar System and the crew believe this is to enable Blake to observe the workings of Federation security. However, Blake suddenly announces his intention to take Control, the centre of all Federation computer networks. After debating the point, the crew agree to help.

Blake has already gained the support of Kasabi, a resistance leader on Earth, but before Blake gets to Earth, Kasabi and her rebels are captured by Servalan and Travis. Kasabi's daughter Veron is forced to capture Blake just outside the Forbidden Zone, the heavily guarded centre surrounding the Control complex. Travis and Servalan make Kasabi reveal the location and the call sign which will bring Blake to the rendezvous.

Blake and Gan teleport down and find Veron in a crypt. She explains that the resistance has been broken, but Blake decides to continue with the operation despite this. Avon and Vila teleport down, but Veron betrays them and steals their teleport bracelets locking them in the crypt. At last the group escapes and makes for the Forbidden Zone.

The four members of the Liberator crew make their way through the various defence mechanisms surrounding the computer complex and eventually break into the room which is supposed to house the computer. However, upon entering they discover that the central control room is totally empty. A few seconds after they enter the room, Travis follows with two mutoids. He explains to Blake that the central control room was moved to an unknown location some 30 years before. However, the public are still encouraged to think that Control was indeed on Earth so that rebels like Blake would continue to attack it in the mistaken belief that they were in fact attacking the heart of the Federation.

Before Travis has a chance to kill Blake and the others, Servalan is marched into the room by Veron and Jenna. Jenna had come looking for Blake when he failed to report in, and was able to cross the Forbidden Zone after Travis had the minefield turned off in order to enable his own crossing. Servalan orders Travis to release his prisoners, and Blake and the crew depart.

Although Jenna has teleport bracelets with her, the crew are wary of using them so far underground and begin to make their way to the surface. Travis throws a grenade after them and, in the ensuing explosion, the roof collapses and traps Gan, who dies. Blake and the others escape and return to the Liberator, aware of their own vulnerability.

## SERIES B EPISODE 6
## TRIAL

Travis is on trial at Space Headquarters for the massacre of some 1400 unarmed civilians – a trial which has been rigged by Servalan so that Travis will be found guilty, executed and thus be unable to supply evidence concerning her inability as Supreme Commander to capture Blake.

Blake, meanwhile, is guilt-stricken over the death of Gan and retreats to an uninhabited planet, making sure that the crew cannot find him. He soon discovers that the planet is inhabited after all when he meets a mischievous imp named Zil, who first steals Blake's homing beacon and teleport bracelet before trying to explain the complex life patterns that exist on the planet. It becomes evident that the planet is itself alive and Zil merely a parasite. The oceans of the planet are organic and are rising rapidly in order to reduce the number of such parasites on the surface. Before long Zil falls into the planet's interior and is 'absorbed'. Threatened with a similar fate, Blake springs back into action and avoids 'capture' long enough for the crew of Liberator to disobey earlier orders, locate him and teleport him back.

Travis is defending himself at his trial, arguing that his action was a direct result of his training as a Federation officer. The three judges are worried and retire. . . .

Having overcome his guilt feelings Blake decides to revive the legend of his crew's invincibility by carrying out a raid on Space Headquarters using Avon's cloaking device as a cover. They hit the space station just as Travis is pronounced guilty. As the emergency shutters close Travis escapes, unhindered by Servalan, who allows him to take a ship piloted by mutoids in order to continue (unofficially) the search for Blake.

## SERIES B  EPISODE 7
## KILLER

Blake is still anxious to be able to intercept Federation messages and needs the T–P Crystal to break their codes. On Fosforon there is not only a crystal but also Tynus, an old ally upon whom Avon presses his claim of calling in an old debt. Avon and Vila teleport to the planet.

Whilst waiting for Avon and Vila to make contact with Tynus on the base and so set up the theft of the crystal, Blake and the others watch the salvage of a 700-year-old space ship. Cally gets a feeling that despite its age, the ship is very dangerous.

Blake sends a warning to the planet, and then teleports down to meet Dr Bellfriar, under whose supervision the dissection of one of the bodies found on the ship will take place. During the autopsy the body comes briefly to life and kills the pathologist. A virulent plague then breaks out on the base.

Meanwhile despite the lack of enthusiasm of Tynus Avon and Vila steal the crystal under cover of a fire and return to Liberator with the news that Tynus has betrayed them and Servalan is on her way.

Bellfriar confirms Blake in his theory that the outbreak of plague is no accident. It appears that part of the galaxy contains an advanced life form that wishes no contact with mankind. The plague which they have distributed attacks people who have been in space, and thus is used to kill only space travelling humans rather than the entire human race. Because of the plague's virulence, Blake is forced to place a warning beacon around the planet announcing its contamination, thus saving Servalan from certain death.

# SERIES B  EPISODE 8
# HOSTAGE

An unprecedented wave of attacks is launched against the Liberator by a fleet of Federation Pursuit Ships using a cloaking device. Despite damage to the Liberator, the ship escapes from the attack.

A message is then received from the planet Exbar. It is

decoded by Orac and is found to come from Travis, who suggests that as he is now an outlaw like Blake, the two should pool their resources. Furthermore Travis reveals that he has captured Blake's cousin Inga, who will be put to death unless Blake comes to Exbar. Despite strong protests from Avon, Blake decides to go along with Travis's demands and teleports to the planet alone.

Meanwhile Councillor Joban meets with Servalan and expresses the High Council's displeasure at her failure to capture Blake. She then receives a signal informing her that Travis is on Exbar and decides to follow up this message by travelling to the planet herself.

On Exbar Blake meets Inga's father, Ushton, who directs him to the Tower in which Travis has set up his base. Meanwhile Avon impulsively decides to follow Blake down to the surface despite their earlier argument. He takes Vila along to help him but both are soon captured, and it is revealed that Ushton has betrayed Blake and the others in order to protect his daughter. Travis tells Blake that his aim is the capture of the Liberator and of course the death of Blake and his crew. He imprisons Blake, Avon and Vila in an oxygen-thin room in which they begin to suffocate. Vila is then taken out and forced to reveal the way in which the teleport system works. A Crimo is sent to the Liberator, where he captures Jenna and Cally; they however regain the upper hand by teleporting him back into space instead of down to the planet.

Meanwhile, in the Tower, Inga provides a distraction whilst Ushton releases Blake, Avon and Vila. In the ensuing chase on the planet's surface, the Crimos are killed and Travis is left.

Avon reveals that he has sent a message to Servalan saying that Travis was on the surface in the hope that she would then deal with Travis as a criminal. After the Liberator has departed, Servalan does arrive on the planet but agrees to take no action against Travis if he continues to pursue Blake and lead her towards the crew of the Liberator. A deal is struck whereby, if Blake and the others are killed, Travis will be classified officially dead. Servalan concludes, 'There is no-one as free as a dead man'.

## SERIES B  EPISODE 9
## COUNTDOWN

The planet Albian is a Federation colony, but only a small force of Federation officers is left on the planet to control the entire population.

Revolution is held at bay by the Federation's having primed a solium radiation device which if detonated will destroy all life but leave buildings intact. A revolution has taken place nevertheless and the device is activated. One Federation survivor, Space Major Provine, attempts to escape by using a rocket especially provided for this eventuality.

At the moment of the revolution Blake, Avon and Vila have teleported to Albian searching for Provine in the belief that he can inform them of the location of the central computer control system. However, when the Liberator's crew meet the rebels they try to help by investigating the mechanism that controls the solium device. Avon discovers that the detonation device is not itself within the Federation complex and could be anywhere on the planet. Orac is used to pinpoint its location inside one of the polar caps.

Avon then meets Grant, a mercenary who has been helping the Albians organise their revolution and recognises him as an old enemy. However, because of Grant's expertise, it is he who teleports with Avon to the polar cap in order to attempt to dismantle the device.

Meanwhile, Blake searches through the ruins of the Federation base and meets Provine who is killed by Blake. Although Provine informs Blake that central control is now called Star One and gives him the name of the one man who knows its location, he fails to disclose any further information before he dies.

Avon and Grant work to de-activate the radiation device but are hampered by faults in the structure of the building in which it is housed. They have switched on the heating system, starting a melting process which causes large amounts of ice to fall into the room. Grant is trapped and injured by a falling beam. Avon nevertheless succeeds in de-activating the device with just one second to spare.

It is revealed at this time that the dispute between the two men originates in Grant's mistaken belief that Avon left Grant's sister Anna to die at the hands of Federation torturers. Avon explains that this is untrue and that he in fact loved Anna. Their differences are reconciled, and Grant chooses to remain on the planet helping the Albian populace build a free society.

## SERIES B  EPISODE 10
## VOICE FROM THE PAST

The Liberator is on its way to Del 10 where the crew plan to take a rest during their search for Star One, when Blake, under the influence of a telepathic message, suddenly changes course for an isolated asteroid. When the crew try to abort the telepathic link, Blake imprisons them and teleports to the asteroid surface, where he meets the legendary and now heavily bandaged guerilla leader Shivan and the defected Arbiter General of the Federation, Ven Glynd. They inform Blake of a plan to denounce the Federation at a Summit meeting on Atlay with the help of Governor Le Grand, who has been working against the Federation for some time whilst staying in office. The plan is to set up a triumvirate of Le Grand, Blake and Shivan.

Despite the objections of the rest of the crew, the Liberator travels with Shivan and Le Grand to the Summit whilst Avon and Cally work hard to locate and destroy the trigger mechanism which drew Blake to the asteroid and which is still active.

Upon reaching the Atlay Summit, Le Grand, Blake, Vila and Jenna teleport down to the surface whilst Avon and Cally remain on board with Shivan and the transmitting device. Shivan then reveals himself to be Travis in disguise, whilst on Atlay Servalan and guards are waiting for Le Grand and Blake.

Avon eventually destroys the trigger mechanism, releasing Blake from his telepathic trance. Travis is left on the surface of the planet, and the crew escape.

## SERIES B EPISODE 11
## GAMBIT

Docholli is a cyber-surgeon reputed to be the only one who still knows the location of Star One, the new Federation computer control centre. He has been traced to Freedom City, a gambling town outside the Federation. Blake, Jenna and Cally teleport into the city in search of Docholli. Meanwhile Travis has already found him on a freighter and, realising that Blake will soon be on Docholli's trail, decides to wait until Blake turns up in order to kill him. Servalan likewise realises that Docholli's arrival in Freedom City will attract both Blake and Travis, and determines to destroy them both and indeed Freedom City itself, which she regards as degenerate.

Whilst Blake, Jenna and Cally go in search of Docholli around the lower level bars, Vila and Avon discuss life on Freedom City and Avon recalls its reputation for gambling. They succeed in reducing Orac in size so that they can take it down to the planet and beat the gaming computers, thus winning a considerable number of credits in the main casino, the Big Wheel.

The owner of the Big Wheel, Krantor, is also the owner of a large part of Freedom City, and it is he whom Servalan approaches for information on the whereabouts of Docholli and Travis. Krantor puts his underlings onto the job of finding the two men and meanwhile continues to run the casino and its special attraction, an alien known as the Klute who challenges all comers to games of Speed Chess. Anyone beating or drawing with the Klute gains one million credits, whilst anyone defeated is instantly electrocuted.

Whilst Blake, Jenna and Cally continue to search, Vila and Avon, with the help of Orac, win four million credits at the gaming tables. Vila is then drugged and tricked into challenging the Klute at Speed Chess, much to Avon's dismay. Nevertheless, with the help of Orac, Vila manages to win once more.

Blake eventually finds Docholli and, immediately after, Travis, who is anxious for Docholli to execute repairs on his false arm which has been turned into a bomb by Servalan. Whilst working on Travis's arm, Docholli reveals that, contrary to popular belief, he does not know the location of Star One. He admits to having worked on the brains of the technicians who built the control centre, removing from them all knowledge of the location, but he never scanned their brain patterns whilst inducing the amnesia. However, he did fake the final operation, thus leaving one man with the memory of the location of Star One.

Blake helps Docholli escape from Servalan and returns to the Liberator to carry on the search for Star One, leaving Travis with one arm unusable because of the bomb mechanism placed there by Servalan. Blake arrives back with Jenna and Cally only seconds after Avon and Vila return with their winnings, which they quickly hide.

# SERIES B EPISODE 12
## THE KEEPER

Continuing their search for Star One, the crew of the Liberator visit the planet Goth, where according to Docholli the one man to know its location has settled. They have also been told that the key to Star One's location is in a brain print attached to an amulet worn by a member of the royal family of Goth.

Blake, Jenna and Vila teleport to the surface but are attacked at once by the tribal inhabitants of Goth. Despite repeated requests for help from Liberator, this does not come – Avon having taken the Liberator out of orbit in order to attack Travis' ship. This he successfully destroys, but Travis has already been transferred to the surface. By the time the Liberator returns, only Blake remains free to teleport back up.

On the surface Vila and Jenna become the property of Gola, the Charl, or chief, of the Goths. Jenna becomes betrothed to the Charl, whilst Vila becomes his jester. However Vila displeases the ruler and is thrown into prison. It is now revealed that Servalan too is on Goth with Travis and is also searching for the brain print which will reveal the location of Star One.

Upon returning to the planet, Blake meets Gola's brother Rod, whom he frees from Gola's men. Rod agrees to help Blake in the rescue of Jenna and Vila, and it seems that he has reasons of his own for wishing to fight Gola. It emerges that although Rod, Gola and Gola's sister Tara are all members of the royal family and each wears an amulet, none of these has a brain print attached to it.

Rod and Gola fight. Gola wins but is poisoned by Tara, who reveals that there is another member of the royal family still alive, their father who was thrown into prison by Gola and Rod many years before. Blake and the others find him dying in prison, but the brain print attached to his amulet has already been removed by

Travis, who has stolen Servalan's ship and fled the planet. As he dies, Gola's father states enigmatically that, 'A fool knows everything and nothing'. Blake repeats this statement, and it triggers a mechanism within the brain of the old man's jester, who was thrown into prison with him. In a hypnotic trance the jester gives full details of the location of Star One. The crew surmise that Lurgen, the surgeon who had the knowledge of Star One, implanted it in the jester's mind, with the old king's phrase as the only trigger mechanism. Armed with this information, the crew leave for Star One.


## SERIES B EPISODE 13
## STAR ONE

It is becoming clear that Star One is breaking down — more and more planets find their climate control systems failing and major space accidents are occurring through computer errors. Servalan at first refuses to accept this but eventually assigns all her resources to the search for Star One. She simultaneously announces her rejection of the power of President and Council and herself takes over as President.

Servalan reveals that, after Star One was built, a group of conditioned technicians remained there to service the computers. It appears, however, that all technicians except one have been taken over by aliens from Andromeda in preparation for a galactic invasion.

The Liberator journeys past the edge of the galaxy to the location given for Star One and eventually discovers a dying star and a single planet. Beyond them is a massive anti-matter minefield put there, so Orac suggests, by the Federation after a brief engagement with an alien scout ship years before. Despite his understanding that the destruction of Star One will mean millions of deaths throughout the galaxy, Blake determines to push ahead in order to justify all his previous acts of rebellion.

With Blake, Cally and Avon on the planet's surface, Jenna and Vila realise that an alien invasion is indeed under way. Travis has betrayed all mankind to the aliens and is helping them remove the minefield. On meeting Blake, Travis shoots and seriously wounds him before he himself is killed by Avon. The explosive devices which Cally has planted on the base are rapidly removed and Avon and Cally get the injured Blake back to the Liberator. Avon takes command having promised Blake that he would fight the invasion rather than use the Liberator to run. With Vila and Cally Avon prepares to attempt to hold off the Andromedans single-handedly until Servalan's ships arrive.

# SERIES C EPISODE 1
# AFTERMATH

The Liberator suffers such severe damage during its attempt to hold off the Andromedan fleet that Zen is forced to shut down life support systems. The crew escape in one-man capsules, each ending up on a different planet. Avon is injured before he is able to escape and Cally places him in a capsule with Orac.

His capsule lands on Sarran in an area where the tribesmen, led by Chel, believe the space battle to be the culmination of one of their prophecies which includes the killing of all survivors. However Dayna saves Avon with bow and arrow. She takes him to the space ship, now buried under the sea, in which she and her father, Hal Mellanby, have been living for twenty years. Before they can reach the ship, Servalan appears and demands to be taken to safety as well.

It appears that Mellanby is himself a fugitive, having led a revolt against the administration on Earth some fifteen years before Blake's time. Like Blake, he was the only one to survive when the guards came down on his rebellion. Avon informs Mellanby of Servalan's identity. Mellanby has been following the war communications and tells Avon that the Federation has won the battle, although Star One has been destroyed and most of the fleet obliterated. Avon is also shown the wide range of weapons that Mellanby, Dayna and Lauren, his adopted daughter, have developed.

Avon uses Orac to contact Zen and arrange for a pick up. Zen reports that an unidentified craft has come alongside the Liberator. Avon instructs the computer to let the ship land, as it might be Vila or Cally making their way back.

Mellanby and his daughter drive off the Sarrans who have attacked the entry lock to the ship in anger at having been deprived of the deaths of Avon and Servalan. When Lauren stays on watch to see if any of the tribesmen return, she is captured and killed. Whilst the others sleep Servalan attempts to steal Orac, and when interrupted by Mellanby puts his vision enhancer out of operation and guns down the blind man, thus escaping with the computer.

Avon and Dayna follow and are forced to rescue Servalan from the Sarrans in order to discover the whereabouts of Orac. With each side trying to double-cross the other, Avon eventually gains the upper hand; however, he and Dayna are teleported before Dayna can kill Servalan. Upon re-boarding Liberator, they are confronted by Tarrant, dressed as a Space Captain, who claims the Liberator is his.

## SERIES C EPISODE 2
## POWERPLAY

Avon and Dayna have escaped from Sarran with Orac only to find the Liberator in the hands of Federation Space Captain Tarrant and Section Leader Klegg. The ship is being flown by Zen with the aim of picking up the crew, and Tarrant and Klegg find they cannot control it without one of the original crew ordering the computer to recognise the new voices. Suspecting that Avon may be one of the former crew, they order him to speak to Zen, but as Avon seems ready to draw a weapon Tarrant knocks him out before he can speak.

Vila is on the planet Chenga and makes constant attempts to communicate with Zen, complaining of the danger and a broken arm. He is rescued first by savages and then by two Hi Techs who are out hunting the primitives for the alleged purpose of reintroducing them to civilised society.

Cally has been picked up by a Hi Tech hospital ship which has also rescued Servalan and is en route for Chenga. By the time it arrives, Vila is in the hospital as well, and the three meet up.

On the Liberator, Avon and Dayna escape Tarrant and discover that someone else on board is killing off Federation guards. In fact it is Tarrant, himself an outlaw. He allies himself with Avon, and they trick Klegg's men and win back the ship.

Whilst Servalan demands and gets transport off Chenga, Cally and Vila discover that they have been deceived – the Hi Techs hunt primitives and the injured from the Intergalactic war to get human organs for spare part surgery on their hospital ships. The two are teleported on board Liberator just as the nurses prepare to exterminate them.

## SERIES C EPISODE 3
## VOLCANO

Having taken Dayna and Tarrant on board, the crew of Liberator seek a permanent base from which to oppose the Federation. They choose the strategically placed Obsidian, on which Dayna has contacts. The populace of the planet are pacifists, and non-aggression has been bred into everyone but the leader Hower and his son Bershar through advanced forms of behavioural psychology. They thus refuse to grant the request for a base for Liberator, nor will they protect the crew against Servalan's forces, who are expected to attack at any time.

At that very moment Servalan is in fact moving her ships into position to attack Liberator, and it is evident that someone has betrayed the Liberator's crew, against all the traditions of Obsidian.

This turns out to be Bershar, who takes Dayna and Tarrant prisoner and gives their teleport bracelets to Mori, Servalan's commander. Mori seizes the Liberator but is beaten off, although he takes Orac and Cally with him when he teleports back down to the planet.

Discovering what has happened, Hower kills his son and frees Dayna and Tarrant. They in turn rescue Cally and Orac. Only then is it found that past invasions of Obsidian have been held at bay through a thermo-nuclear device buried in the massive volcano which dominates the planet. Recognising that Servalan is about to attack, Hower orders the destruction of the planet rather than accept any form of domination.

## SERIES C EPISODE 4
## DAWN OF THE GODS

Whilst flying under the control of Zen the Liberator makes an unexpected course change. Despite Orac's insistence that everything on the ship is behaving quite normally, the Liberator continues to be pulled off course. Eventually it is recognised that the ship is being pulled into a black hole. Orac has failed to prevent this because it is fascinated by the unusual properties exhibited by this particular black hole and wants a closer look. As the ship goes out of control, Avon tries to save himself by putting on a spacesuit. Tarrant stops him in the irrational desire that everyone should die together.

The crew recover consciousness to find that they have in fact not been destroyed and that the ship is still intact although no stars can be seen on Zen's monitoring system. Vila is sent through a hatch to investigate what lies outside the ship and discovers that the Liberator has in fact landed on Crandor, an artificial planet ruled by Lord Thaarn, a creature who figures in the fairy tales of Auron. Thaarn has constructed a series of gravity generators with which he captures passing ships to strip of their Herculanium. This is then used to add to the power of the generators, with which Thaarn aims to gain mastery of the galaxy. The Thaarn is a member of an advanced life form that visited Auron thousands of years before. The creature recognises Cally as an Auron telepath and wishes to share its loneliness and conquest with her.

The crew are set to work on Crandor developing calculations for the gravity generators. However Orac is left on board and foils all attempts by Thaarn's men to retrieve it and to dismantle the ship. Cally tricks the Thaarn into turning off the control field for a moment, and the crew take advantage of this opportunity to escape from the planet. The Thaarn also escapes before the planet explodes.


# SERIES C EPISODE 5
# THE HARVEST OF KAIROS

Servalan launches a planned attack on the Liberator, using a special flight formation which Tarrant recognises. Tarrant begins to evade the attack whilst, in her headquarters, news comes to Servalan of a construction worker who is speaking openly of her inability to take the Liberator. This underling turns out to be Jarvik, a former Space Commander who had resigned his commission because of his disaffection with the Federation's dependence on high technology. He boasts that he could take the Liberator with three ships, and Servalan agrees to let him try.

Meanwhile, Avon has become totally distracted by an odd, immobile, rock-like life form called Sopron. He thus takes no part in either the evasion of Servalan's forces under the guidance of Jarvik or the plan by Tarrant to steal Kairopan — a valuable crystal available on Kairos for just one week every fifteen years. All appears to go smoothly with the theft until the crates of crystal harvested by the Federation are moved into the Liberator, when guards reveal themselves and capture the ship and its crew.

In an attempt to salvage the situation, Avon

manipulates Zen so that Servalan, who takes over Liberator, is forced to put the crew down on a habitable planet instead of killing them immediately. However Servalan fulfils the bargain by teleporting Avon and his colleagues to Kairos. Since the one week in which the Kairopan can be harvested safely has passed, the planet is now in a phase deadly to human life although there is no information about the nature of the threat.

Servalan gives Jarvik a further challenge, to remove the teleport bracelets from Avon, Tarrant and the others, now on Kairos. As he does this, Jarvik tells Avon that the reason no human life can exist on Kairos after the week of harvest is that large insect-like creatures seek out the Kairopan and use it to spin silk. Anyone who has even touched the substance will be attacked, and since the Kairopan is so exceptionally valuable no humans on the planet can ever resist it.

Meanwhile Avon has discovered an ancient space ship which appears to be workable although only designed for very short journeys into space. Despite his misgivings, Tarrant manages to fly the ship, and Avon then plugs in an analogue version of the Sopron rock which convinces Zen on the Liberator that it is viewing a space ship of slightly greater size, slightly greater speed and slightly greater weaponry capacity than Liberator.

Despite Jarvik's protestations, Servalan is tricked by this ruse and teleports off the Liberator. Tarrant then lands the small spacecraft alongside the Liberator and the crew regain control. In the final moments, Jarvik is mistakenly killed by one of Servalan's guards.

## SERIES C EPISODE 6
## THE CITY AT THE EDGE OF THE WORLD

Tarrant has negotiated a deal with the inhabitants of an uncharted planet known as Keezarn – in return for unspecified services from Vila, crystals will be provided for the weaponry system on Liberator. Vila is particularly reluctant to go down and only acquiesces when Tarrant bullies him into submission. He teleports to the surface but fails to take a tracer by which the crew can monitor his whereabouts. Cally teleports down after Vila to collect the box of crystals, and discovers that the box contains only a bomb. She escapes and, unable to locate Vila, returns to the ship. Avon and Cally then teleport down in order to search for Vila.

Vila is met by two natives who refuse to speak to him but lead him to an ancient deserted city. There, among others, he meets Bayban the Butcher, the Federation's most wanted criminal, and Kerril, a female gunfighter. Bayban believes he has found a room in which all the treasures of the planet are stored. However the door to the room is secured and Bayban has been unable to open it. He therefore orders Vila to set to work on it, and Vila soon discovers that the vault is protected by a force wall, not a door. This he opens.

Kerril and Vila have become attracted to each other, and she goes with him through the barrier into the vault beyond. They make their way through a series of passages until they enter an instant transportation mechanism which takes them to a star ship 3,000 light years distant. A message is broadcast to Vila and Kerril explaining that the builder of the system had lived on Keezarn thousands of years before, when the planet was at the height of its economic, political and technological growth. Foreseeing an inevitable decline into barbarism, the ship had been pre-programmed to travel through space seeking a planetary system which the people of Keezarn could colonise and hence rebuild their civilisation. The belief was that if a suitable system could be found with more than one planet for colonisation, a second return to barbarism could be avoided. The matter transmitter, it is explained, was sealed into the vault so that it could only be opened from time to time. A genetically engineered message had been programmed into the race memory of the population so that they would feel the need to get someone to open the vault every thirty-five generations.

Vila and Kerril understand that the matter transmitter will not return them to Keezarn; further, they only have enough oxygen to exist on the space ship for a short while. Thinking that they will soon die, the two lie down on the couches and make love.

Meanwhile, Avon and Cally have captured some of Bayban's men and question them. They subsequently bring down the rest of the crew of the Liberator to try and rescue Vila. At the same time Vila and Kerril find that their ship has actually landed, although due to a malfunction of the force field the door leading out cannot be opened. Vila breaks through the force field and finds himself on a beautiful planet suitable for colonisation. Whilst he and Kerril are inventing names for the planet, he comes upon the crystals which he had originally been sent to Keezarn to obtain. This breaks the spell between the lovers and makes Vila feel that they should go back to the city at once, much to Kerril's dismay.

Meanwhile, the Liberator's crew capture Bayban and discover the secret of the door, through which Vila and Kerril dramatically reappear. Norl, the leader of the people of Keezarn, then takes his people through to the matter transmitter in order to lead them to their new planet. Whilst Vila is deciding whether to join Kerril on the new planet and spend the rest of his life there, Bayban breaks free from custody and threatens both Vila and Kerril. Vila quickly ushers Kerril and Norl into the vault, which closes behind them leaving Vila no choice but to return to the Liberator. He does so as Bayban tries to blast his way into the vault with a laser cannon which destroys the whole city. Back on board the Liberator, Vila surprises the crew by producing the crystals he had been sent down to get, and is left with his sadness over the loss of Kerril.

# SERIES C EPISODE 7
# CHILDREN OF AURON

Servalan launches a plan against Auron which will wipe out its entire population. The plan takes advantage of the isolation Auron has practised in recent years which has left its populace susceptible to plagues from ouside. In order to introduce the virus that figures in her plan, Servalan captures an Auron space ship, infects the pilot and sends him back to his home base to spread the disease. Then when the distress call goes out, she answers it and prepares a drug which will overcome the plague.

On the Liberator, Avon wishes to visit Earth to revenge the death of his girlfriend, Anna Grant, but this plan is aborted when Cally receives a telepathic message from her twin Zelda informing her of the situation of Auron. The Liberator makes for the planet.

The true nature of Servalan's plan becomes clear: she wishes both to capture the Liberator (counting on Cally's return to Auron in its hour of need) and to use the cloning process developed on Auron in order to create children in her image. Servalan's officers kill a group of Auronar who come to her ship to be cured of the disease. They then use their suits to return to Auron and take over its base, where they capture Tarrant, Avon and Cally, who are already on the base trying to help.

Using her telepathic powers, Zelda helps rescue the crew of Liberator, who escape to the Bio-Replication plant in the faith that Servalan will not risk destroying her own children. Once there, a plan is devised for Clinician Franton to take enough genetic material to clone 5,000 individuals and thus save the race. She is teleported up to the Liberator with everyone except Zelda, who stays to adjust the Replication Plant.

Meanwhile one of Servalan's officers, anxious for promotion, tricks the Supreme Commander into believing that the genetic banks have been switched and her genes are not being replicated on Auron. She therefore gives the order to destroy the plant, only to feel the death of her children as the bombs hit. Cally likewise senses the death of Zelda. But the genetic stock of the race of the Auronar is saved and transported to another planet whilst Servalan kills off two of her officers.

## SERIES C EPISODE 8
## RUMOURS OF DEATH

Avon decides to hunt down once and for all the person responsible for the death of his girlfriend Anna Grant. She had been killed after she had helped him in his attempt to break the Federation banking cartel and commit the biggest theft in the history of the galaxy. His plan involves returning to Earth, getting caught and then holding out until he is confronted by Shrinker, the hardest of all Federation interrogators and the person he believes caused Anna's death.

At the moment Shrinker appears in his cell, Avon turns off a transmitter which has been constantly beaming his position to Liberator, bringing down a rescue party from the ship who teleport the two men back. After cleaning himself up, Avon takes Shrinker to an underground cavern and confronts him with a picture of Anna. Shrinker convinces Avon that he knew nothing of her death. In fact, throughout the entire operation, Avon is told, it was thought he was running a political movement; therefore a top officer code-named 'Bartolomew' was watching Avon constantly and arrested anyone he even looked at.

In Residence One, Servalan is preparing an official reception. Councillor Chesku is out taking a walk with his wife Sula (who, as the pictures make clear, is Anna Grant). Whilst the Councillor practises his speech, two men disguised as Federation troopers appear and confront him. When he tries to escape, Sula shoots him in the back.

Avon leaves Shrinker in the cavern with no means of escape, merely a gun with which to commit suicide. He determines to find Servalan, the only person who would know Bartolomew's identity. At this same moment Sula's plan to take over the Presidency is coming to fruition with a raid on the presidential residence. By the time Avon and the others find Servalan, she is chained in a dungeon. Whilst they are questioning her, Sula appears and Avon recognises her at once. With the information given him by Shrinker, he now sees that the only person Bartolomew could have been was Anna herself. When Servalan confirms this Anna moves to draw a weapon, but Avon shoots first and kills her. Whilst holding Anna in his arms Servalan moves to kill Avon, but he is teleported back to Liberator before Servalan can complete the task, and she is rescued by loyal troops.

## SERIES C EPISODE 9
## SARCOPHAGUS

The Liberator is in deep space and the crew are contemplating mining an asteroid for some rare minerals, when an alien space ship of totally unknown design drifts into detector range. It appears to be unmanned and has a strange effect upon Cally. She denies that she is receiving any signal from the ship, and along with Avon and Vila teleports across to the craft to investigate. They discover a corpse laid out in what appears to be some ceremonial splendour, and also a mechanism that Cally automatically picks up.

On the Liberator, Dayna and Tarrant are informed that there is a dangerous build-up of energy on the alien ship. They pass this information on to Avon, who demands to be teleported back immediately. However, in what appears to be a teleportation malfunction, only Cally arrives on the ship carrying the alien artefact. In desperation, Cally teleports back, links hands with Avon and Vila, and brings them back to the Liberator just seconds ahead of an explosion on the alien craft.

Without the others knowing, Cally has also brought back a ring from the alien craft. Strange things begin to happen on the Liberator, including a build-up of static electricity, and Cally appears to be acting in an unusual way under the influence of the artefact. She eventually reactivates the object, which glows rapidly before crumbling into dust. At that moment, an alien being appears on the Liberator, draining power from Cally and beginning to appear somewhat in her form. Power is also being drained from the Liberator. Zen and Orac both cease to function.

Having attacked various members of the crew, the alien turns on Avon. He, however, stands up to her demands for servitude and taunts her to do her worst and kill him. She retreats from this final possibility, clearly wanting his service rather than his death. Avon finally takes the ring from the alien and, in facing up to her, forces Cally to fight off the alien influence and regain full consciousness. Together they defeat and destroy the alien, but not before she reveals that her home is many centuries distant on a world totally unknown to humans. She tells them that her kind, who remain unnamed throughout the episode, know what death is like and through death remain aware of the passing years whilst being deaf, dumb, blind and totally unable to move. It is in order to end this torment of living death that the alien has sought to gain Cally's body.

## SERIES C EPISODE 10
## ULTRAWORLD

The crew of Liberator pick up some unusual readings, the

74

source of which is identified as a planet of a type totally unknown to them. They conclude that it has been built by an alien race with a technology far in advance of Mankind's. Avon is interested in finding out the reason for the planet's existence. The others express misgivings but agree to take the Liberator to within 1,000 spacials.

While the rest of the crew get some rest Cally, who is left alone, becomes influenced by a force emanating from the planet. When the others return to the flight deck, they find she has teleported to the planet. Her faint calls for help are heard on the communication system, and Avon, Tarrant and Dayna teleport down to the planet, leaving Vila with Orac on the ship.

They discover that Ultraworld is in fact a giant computer which they are inside. They meet the three Ultra, who state that their function is to gather information. They insist that Cally is receiving treatment for mental shock and Avon, Tarrant and Dayna are taken to see her. It becomes clear that all is not well with Cally, and Tarrant discovers that the Ultra wipe the memories from the minds of new species they meet and place them in special containers, where they become part of the Ultra's store of knowledge. The bodies are then either fed into the Core of Ultraworld so that the clean brain can help expand its power, or the bodies are retained intact for use as menials. Thus although it is true that the Ultra do gather information for their massive Library, they have an over-riding function to serve the Core, which must grow in order to live.

Cally and Avon both have their brains wiped clean by the Ultra, and Cally is rescued just as she is about to be fed into the Core. Tarrant and Dayna take Cally back to where Avon is being stored. After a series of battles with the Ultra and the menials, they reverse the process through which the brains have been wiped clean. Tarrant is forced to guess which memory tube relates to which person, but fortunately all is well and the correct mind enters the correct body.

Meanwhile, the Core is experiencing high levels of disturbance emanating from the Liberator, which has by now been brought into storage within Ultraworld. It is this continuing distraction that has allowed the crew to escape, and in the continuous build-up of problems, they are able to rejoin Vila on board the Liberator. The disturbance, they find, was caused by Vila and Orac working together. Vila had been teaching Orac riddles which the computer then used to confuse the Core, since it was only ready to absorb logical impulses from the brain. Having accomplished this, Orac then directed the Core's own emissions back at itself so that, as the Liberator flies off from Ultraworld, the Core finally explodes and destroys the entire planet.

# SERIES C EPISODE 11
# MOLOCH

The Liberator is following Servalan's space ship and its crew are puzzled by the fact that the cruiser is not only on its own, but heading across uncharted space at the very edge of the galaxy. It suddenly disappears, and when the Liberator follows the crew find themselves plunging towards an unknown planet. They manage to escape the pull of the planet and find that once again it is no longer visible. The planet is named Sardos and is contained within an energy barrier that makes it invisible from space. It follows that in order to be able to generate this barrier, the Sardoans must have an exceptionally advanced technology, and the crew fear the fact that Servalan may gain access to this technology.

Tarrant therefore wishes to go down to the planet, but is prevented from doing so immediately by the fact that the teleport will not operate through the barrier, both barrier and teleport operating on similar wavelengths. Orac suggests that Tarrant could instead teleport into a hollow bulkhead on a passing space ship. He accepts this suggestion and teleports with Vila, but Vila is placed outside the bulkhead due to a mistake in co-ordinates. He is quickly discovered and befriended by Doran, who reveals that the ship is full of convicts from a nearby Federation penal colony. The convicts were recently liberated and have been recruited for a renegade force on Sardos under the command of Grose.

Once on the planet, Vila is found by Tarrant and expresses his continuing disaffection with Tarrant's plans. Tarrant threatens him with a gun, and Vila leaves and throws in his lot with Doran.

Meanwhile, Servalan meets Grose and Lector, two survivors from the Federation fleet engaged in the Intergalactic War. It turns out that both are deserters, having killed most of their superior officers and retained one in suspended animation. They have done this with the aid of the immensely advanced technology of the planet, which includes machines capable of transmuting matter and duplicating anything using pure energy. Some of the machines are so vast that they can be used to replicate whole space ships, and it becomes clear that the convicts Grose is gathering are to become pilots of the new ships. Servalan, it appears, has been trapped into coming to the planet so that Grose and Lector can use her space ship as the model for a completely new fleet. They also feel that they can make use of the technology to analyse the brain patterns of space commanders, and so make automatic systems to fly their ships upon simple verbal instructions from the human pilots.

On board the Liberator, Cally modifies the teleport so that it will work through the force field. Avon and Dayna go down to the planet and are quickly captured. Meanwhile, Doran mistakenly thinks that Vila needs a woman to cheer him up, and finds him one: Servalan. She tricks Vila, escapes, finds her imprisoned space commanders and release them, killing a number of other imprisoned people and inadvertently releasing Tarrant.

Tarrant and Vila team up once again and, with the help of a Sardoan and Doran, find and release Avon and Dayna. Grose and Lector are killed by Doran, but at that moment Moloch, the computer which is at the centre of much of the high technology of the planet, comes into its own and appears to kill Doran and the Sardoan. Moloch is revealed to be a creature from the future created by the transmutation machines on the basis of computer projection of what their population will look like in two million years' time. Moloch has in fact become the supreme power on Sardos. He wishes to procure the Liberator in order to travel the galaxy, and he tricks Cally into teleporting him on board. However, he assumes erroneously that his life support system is an integral part of himself – the teleport recognises only Moloch as living matter, and without his ancillary machinery he instantly dies. Avon uses the transmutation machine to create more teleport bracelets and the crew return to the Liberator, leaving Servalan to escape with her freed crew.

## SERIES C EPISODE 12
## DEATH WATCH

Wanting a break from the endless battle with the Federation, Vila gets Orac to tell the crew of Liberator that they need a rest. When the news comes of a dispute between the United Planets of Teal and the Vandor Confederacy of Planets, the crew decide to take advantage of this situation and visit the scene of the dispute at which outsiders are treated as honoured guests.

The two systems (both outside the Federation) avoid fighting bloody wars by agreeing to each have a First Champion. When war is declared the Champions of each fight a battle on a site set and maintained by a computer. Many different possible sites exist, and the computer makes its selection randomly. To increase public appreciation of the battle, the Champions have sensors implanted in their brains, the signals from which are boosted by the computer so that they can be received by anyone with a small receiver affixed to the forehead. The whole operation is watched by an arbiter from each of the warring systems and another neutral arbiter who looks out for any infractions of the Teal-Vandor Convention.

On this occasion the declaration of war comes as something of a surprise, and matters take on a more sinister complexion when it is revealed that the 'neutral' arbiter is Servalan, who just happens to have a war-fleet massed on the borders of the two systems. What is more, one of the combatants is Tarrant's brother Deeta.

Now certain that there is a plot under way, Avon asks Tarrant to share his brother's experiences as Champion of Teal and Dayna those of Vinni, the Champion of Vandor. In a brief shoot-out Deeta is killed, but both Tarrant and Dayna realise that something is wrong. Orac suggests that Vinni is an android – a clear breach of the Convention. Avon suggests that were this breach to be disclosed (through Servalan's demand for a physical examination of the contestants, which as neutral arbiter she is entitled to ask for) real war would break out and the Federation would move in and annex both systems.

Dayna teleports to the arbiters' room and stops the medical examination whilst Tarrant takes up the option of challenging Vinni by right of blood feud. Using Orac to tap the central computer, Tarrant learns the exact position of the new combat, makes ready and, despite his hesitation to shoot the android in the back, does in the end shoot him down.

With the death of both Champions a new ritual war has to be fought, but when Tarrant hears that he is the new First Champion of Teal he decides to leave rapidly.

# SERIES C EPISODE 13
# TERMINAL

Avon has taken the Liberator on a course of which the others know nothing and refuses to discuss the matter. His behaviour is becoming so extreme that the rest of the crew let him have the flight deck entirely to himself for some thirty hours. It becomes apparent both that no one will be able to countermand any of Avon's instructions to Zen, and that Avon is himself following a set of complex instructions which are being relayed to him.

As the ship progresses towards its final destination, a mass of fluid particles is encountered which Avon, despite protestations from the crew, decides to fly straight through. The particles have the immediate effect of knocking out the ship's hull sensors, but no other effects are obvious to the crew.

The ship eventually arrives at Terminal, an artificial egg-shaped planet created by pre-Federation Earth scientists and put into the orbit of Mars. It was long thought destroyed, and no explanation is available for its sudden appearance in this part of the galaxy. Following instructions, Avon teleports down, giving stern warnings that the rest of the crew are not to come after him. He says he has left a message with Zen explaining what he has been up to. He also tells them to leave the area should he fail to report back every hour on the hour. Despite these warnings, Tarrant and Cally teleport down and attempt to follow him.

On the Liberator, Vila and Dayna realise that something is going seriously wrong as major system breakdowns begin to occur. The particles through which the Liberator has passed are simply eating the Liberator away. On Terminal, Avon is directed towards an underground complex. Throughout his approach he is shadowed by a man and woman, but before they can join him they are attacked by two Links, ferocious ape-like creatures. Tarrant and Cally are likewise attacked but manage to kill the Links and follow Avon down into the interior of the planet. Once inside, Avon discovers that Blake appears to be alive, but seriously injured and held prisoner. His injuries would prevent him from teleporting.

On Liberator, Zen is approaching the end of his struggle to stay on line. All final resources are directed towards keeping the teleport system open. The rest of the ship becomes inactive.

Despite the fact that he seems to have seen Blake, it becomes clear that Servalan had sent Avon a simulated message from Blake in which he claimed to have discovered a vast hoard of wealth which he offered to share with Avon. Servalan was also responsible for the auto-suggestive hypnosis which caused Avon to 'see' the image of an injured Blake. She reveals her purpose in setting this trap – to gain the Liberator once and for all – and just as Avon is refusing to send a message for the rest of the Liberator's crew to join him, the captive Tarrant and Cally are brought in. Servalan persuades Tarrant to have Vila teleport Dayna down and so is able to take over the Liberator at last.

Once they are on board the Liberator, Servalan's aide teleports Vila down to the surface. Vila, at the last moment, grabs Orac on the pretence that it is 'a pile of junk' he built for his own amusement. Servalan instructs her new crew to take the Liberator out of orbit, but as she does so the ship begins to break up. Avon is left with the awareness that he has lost the Liberator and failed to find Blake or the treasure promised by him. Also feeling the results of Avon's failures and recklessness, the rest of the crew start the search for a way off the planet Terminal.

# SERIES D  EPISODE 1
## RESCUE

Having lost the Liberator and become stranded on the planet Terminal, Dayna and Avon go out in search of the space ship which Servalan has informed them she has left on the planet for them. However before they can enter the ship, they notice a Link making its way onto the ship. The animal triggers a set of explosive devices as it enters, thus destroying the ship and apparently the only method of escape left for the stranded crew. Dayna and Avon make their way back to the underground living quarters, but before they can get there further massive explosions wreck the underground areas. Vila escapes and, in a rare display of heroics, rescues Tarrant. Before he can return to rescue Cally also, the hatchway leading to the interior of the planet closes and there are further explosions. Avon goes back later and discovers that Cally is dead, but he does manage to bring out a somewhat battered Orac.

Whilst making their way to the relative safety of higher ground, the crew are met by Dorian, who claims to be a salvage operator. Suspecting Dorian from the outset, Avon pulls a gun on him and forces him to lead the crew back to his space ship, Scorpio. Although looking like a very ordinary planet-hopper, the ship contains a variety of sophisticated modifications which make the crew even more suspicious. Scorpio takes off under Tarrant's guidance and then, under automatic control, takes the crew to the planet Xenon.

There they meet Dorian's associate Soolin, who has clearly been expecting their arrival. Whilst the crew are resting, Dorian removes part of the mechanism of their weapons and then pulls a gun on Avon, to whom he reveals the secret of the planet. He claims to have discovered a room deep within the planet that has strange properties which act in such a way as to keep Dorian permanently young and also remove any signs of the life that he leads. During his thus much prolonged life, Dorian has undertaken the modifications they have noticed on the space ship and its computer, and has been working on a teleportation system which he has yet to perfect.

It becomes obvious that one of his reasons for rescuing the crew of the Liberator was to get his hands on Orac, which he trusts will be able to solve the problems of the teleportation system for him. His other plan is to take the crew to his underground room, where they will be absorbed into a creature known as Gestalt. This creature was originally Dorian's partner, but has since absorbed a number of other humans in order to perpetuate the properties of the room. Dorian hopes that when Gestalt absorbs the entire crew of the Liberator plus his own colleague Soolin, it will give him much-needed extra strength.

Meanwhile Vila, who has escaped the attention of Dorian, manages to find a loaded gun and at the last moment pass it to Avon, who destroys the creature and thus destroys Dorian. In the final scene, Dorian dissolves into dust whilst the creature returns to the shape of his former partner.

# SERIES D EPISODE 2
# POWER

Having killed Dorian, the survivors of the Liberator discover that they can no longer get back to the space ship Scorpio because of a well-protected door which Vila is unable to open. Escape becomes a matter of urgency when they discover that they have only a limited period of time to get onto the ship before the explosion of a device which has been preset by Dorian and which it seems can only be stopped by Dorian himself.

On the planet's surface, the final stages of a war between the Hommiks and the Seska are being waged. The Hommiks are male-dominated and the Seska are

83

totally female. The Hommiks have been winning the war for many years, and the Seska are reduced to three women. In the past, the Seska were helped to survive by Dorian, who had used Scorpio to provide nutrients for their food-processing plant.

Initially Avon and later Tarrant, Vila and Dayna are captured by the Hommiks, who retain remnants of the high technology developed by their civilisation before its destruction by war. Whilst the Hommiks appear to have lost contact with most of their past, the Seska have survived through the use of controlled telekinetic powers.

Avon and the other survivors of Liberator make their various escapes from the Hommiks, but Avon recognises that the leader of the Seska is not telling the full truth in her explanations of what has been happening. He realises, for example, that she has not been working on a plan to develop a teleport system, but rather has been seeking to gain control of Scorpio in order to effect her own escape from the planet. Thus her efforts to help Tarrant and the others open the door sealed by Dorian have their ulterior motive and are not governed solely by a desire to get nutrients for the Seska's hydroponic plant.

In order to counteract her deviousness, Avon has instructed Orac to be less than straightforward in helping Tarrant, Villa and Dayna. Orac has used the time to work out how a small piece of jewellery worn by the Seska can be used as a teleport system and effectively succeeds in grasping this. The one remaining Seska teleports to Scorpio, but is killed by Avon who then teleports the others on board. Just as Vila is about to teleport he is joined by Soolin who demands to go with the rest of the crew, a demand which is accepted.

## SERIES D  EPISODE 3
## TRAITOR

Avon and the crew of Scorpio are concerned about the continuing rapid expansion of the Federation. When they hear that one of the latest conquests is Helotrix they become even more concerned, remembering the Helots' past resistance against the Federation. They therefore visit the planet, and Tarrant and Dayna are teleported to the surface in order to discover what secret weapon the Federation is using to subjugate the population. The resistance on the planet is run by Hunda, who when contacted by Tarrant and Dayna, explains that the Federation is using a new drug, Pylene 50, which pacifies everyone who is exposed to it.

Whilst waiting on the ship for Tarrant and Dayna to complete their investigations, Avon instructs Orac to look into the possibility of redesigning parts of the propulsion system of Scorpio in order to make it more effective. However Orac, not wishing to undertake this work itself, passes it over to the nearest suitable computers.

On the surface of the planet, Tarrant and Dayna discuss with Hunda possible ways into the city and also meet Leitz, a Federation officer who is supposedly also a supporter of the resistance movement. What finally becomes clear is that, unknown to his superior commanders, Leitz is working directly under Servalan, who now goes under the name of Commissioner Sleer. In this capacity, he sets out to betray Hunda and his rebels.

Tarrant and Dayna discover the source of Pylene 50 and from its manufacture gain an antidote which they give to the resistance leaders, warning them at the same time of Leitz' double-cross. During the fighting that follows the rebels' raid on the Magnetrix terminal, which is the communications centre of Helotrix, Tarrant and Dayna are amazed to spot Servalan.

Meanwhile a search ship has been launched towards Scorpio. Avon assumes that this is because Tarrant and Dayna have been picked up by security forces; however, he soon discovers what has actually happened – Orac has passed the engine redesign problem on to the nearest available engineering computers, which happen to be the ones on Helotrix. This interference with the Helotrix computers has been spotted by the Helotrix command, and hence the raid.

Avon takes Scorpio down to cloud level and picks up Tarrant and Dayna, who by this time have finished helping the rebels and bring Avon the information that Servalan did not die in the destruction of the Liberator as it orbited the planet Terminal.


# SERIES D  EPISODE 4
# STAR DRIVE

Avon takes Scorpio into a planetary system where precious Selsium Ore can be obtained. However in trying to approach the system under the cover of an asteroid (hence avoiding detection by the Federation), they crash and are rendered immobile. Whilst undertaking repairs, Scorpio is approached by three Federation ships of an unfamiliar type, but these explode suddenly. A slow-motion replay of the events reveals that the explosions were caused by bolts discharged from a single-seater space chopper moving at hitherto unimagined speeds. Orac interprets this as indicating that a certain Dr Plaxton has completed work on the Photonic Drive, and thus they begin a search for Plaxton.

Investigation of the chopper shows that the pilot was one of the Space Rats — psychopaths who love speed and violence — and so, despite Vila's worries, Scorpio travels to Caspar, the Space Rat base. Dayna and Vila are teleported down as unwitting decoys whilst Scorpio lands and the rest of the crew prepare to steal the Drive. Atlan, the Space Rats' leader, has arranged for Dr Plaxton to have all the raw materials she needs to develop the new drive, but the unlikely alliance is breaking down as Plaxton becomes increasingly concerned about the psychotic nature of the Space Rats.

Vila and Dayna are captured by the Space Rats, but try to work their way out of the problem by pretending to be previous students of Dr Plaxton. They further suggest that the star drive machine on Plaxton's bench is less developed than one on which she had previously worked with the 'students', thus ingratiating themselves with the Space Rats, and earning a reprieve.

Tarrant, Avon and Soolin rescue Vila and Dayna and take the prototype drive, along with Dr Paxton. After a cross country chase they escape from the Space Rats and take off in Scorpio, but are quickly pursued by Federation ships. In order to help outrun them Dr Plaxton begins to install the new drive unit, but when it looks like time is running out Avon completes the linkage bringing the drive on line without giving Plaxton time to get clear and escape the effects of the drive. She is thus killed on making the final connection, but the ship outruns the launched plasma bolts.

## SERIES D  EPISODE 6
## ANIMALS

Tarrant and Dayna fly to Bucol 2 with the aim of reaching Justin, an old tutor of Dayna's. As Dayna teleports down, Scorpio comes under attack and Tarrant is forced to return to base using the Star Drive.

On the planet Dayna is faced by grotesque animals, two of which she kills before Justin appears and rescues her. Justin reveals that he has been involved in genetic engineering of the animals — at first during the war under Federation orders and since then of his own volition. The purpose of the experiments has been to create a breed of intelligent creatures able to go into areas of high radiation in order to make them safe for humans without suffering any ill effects themselves. His work is nearly complete — one animal, Og, has already developed enough intelligence to understand language but has broken out of the compound with some others and is refusing to come in even for food.

On Xenon Base, Avon and the others repair Scorpio and prepare to return for Dayna, whilst Servalan (under the name Sleer) is becoming curious about a planet hopper that can move at Time Distort 12 and wonders what it has been doing on Bucol 2. She finds Borr, the one man who knows of the ultra-secret Bucol 2 project, and realises its value in her attempt to claw back power. Borr, however, recognises her, and 'Sleer' decides to have him eradicated.

On Bucol 2, Dayna agrees to help Justin by trying to persuade Og to return to the compound for food. Og panics and pushes Dayna over a cliff, where she is immediately found by a troop of mutoids from Sleer's ship. Under torture Dayna reveals the situation to Servalan, who orders the capture of Og.

Through the use of aversion therapy, Dayna is made to hate Justin and is then returned to his headquarters. There she finds that he has destroyed his work in the belief that the creatures have killed her, whom he has come to love. Dayna, however, now hates Justin and opens the door to the Federation guards, who take him to Sleer. He tells her to find Og, the key to all his work.

Scorpio returns and, with Vila left on board, the crew teleport down to find Dayna. They discover Justin's wrecked workshops and move in to attack the mutoids around Sleer's ship. Whilst this is happening, Dayna is undergoing further therapy to make her love Justin, but as it reaches completion he is killed by Sleer. Og too is caught in the crossfire. Sleer escapes, leaving Dayna to mourn her dead love.

# SERIES D EPISODE 5
# HEADHUNTER

Tarrant and Vila travel to Pharos in order to pick up Muller, a brilliant cyberneticist who studied under Ensor (inventor of Orac) and who has subsequently developed a master android. However before Scorpio can arrive Muller radios that he is in trouble, and Tarrant quickly teleports down to find a dead guard, Muller and a box which seems to disturb the cyberneticist. When Tarrant takes the box back to Scorpio, Muller becomes even more troubled and a struggle ensues. Vila hits Muller, who apparently collapses and dies, while back on Pharos a technician discovers the headless corpse of the real Muller. . . .

Vila and Tarrant put 'Muller' into a cryogenic chamber in the hope of resuscitating him back on Xenon Base, but the ship soon starts to exhibit instrument failure – with even Slave taking on an aggressive attitude. When life support fails, Tarrant and Vila are rescued by means of the teleport despite Orac's order that the ship be isolated and the teleport put out of action.

Avon takes Muller's wife, who is already on Xenon Base, back to Scorpio only to find 'Muller' missing. He then appears on the base and immediately murders his wife. By now it is clear that this is in reality Muller's android who has killed his maker and taken his head in order to gain entry to Scorpio and the base. His eventual object is Orac, with which he plans to control all organic life in the galaxy. However Orac has been concealed from the android by Soolin.

Vila opens the box the android was afraid of and discovers its real head, which contains all the circuits needed to give it a conscience. Using Orac as bait, they lure the android onto a metal bridge on which it is electrocuted. Avon puts the inhibitor head on the android but is knocked out by a powerful discharge. Dayna quickly lays charges and, following Orac's advice, blows up the android to save organic humanoid life from domination by the android plus Orac. Avon recovers and is furious at the destruction, whilst Orac is left to comment on the arrogance of both Avon and Muller.

# SERIES D  EPISODE 7
## ASSASSIN

Vila picks up a strangely coded message from Servalan which is taken to mean that she is hiring the professional killer Cancer to eliminate the crew of Scorpio on the planet Domo. Although Avon has heard of Cancer, he has no idea who he is or what he looks like. Taking Orac's advice he persuades the others to take the battle to Cancer, and they prepare to visit Domo – as does Servalan.

Domo is the headquarters of a band of pirates who capture space ship passengers and sell them into slavery. Avon teleports near to the pirates' base and arranges to be captured. However, the plan goes wrong when he loses his teleport bracelet and is forced to rely on an old slave to retrieve it. From the old man they discover the route taken by Cancer's ship, and following this lead eventually teleport aboard. Cancer is captured and securely bound. Also on board is Piri, a dancer to whom Tarrant is attracted. She appears terrified of Cancer and Tarrant becomes ever more protective of her.

Despite the fact that Cancer has been secured completely, Nebrox is murdered, Soolin just escapes and Avon is captured. Piri reveals herself to be Cancer – the man they took to be the killer was a hired actor and has himself been killed by Piri.

Piri releases a deadly crab onto Avon, but Soolin and Tarrant come to the rescue and the crab kills Piri instead. Servalan, who has been behind the whole scheme, sends her ship to destroy Cancer's, but Scorpio arrives just in time and teleports Tarrant, Avon and Soolin to safety.

# SERIES D  EPISODE 8
## GAMES

Both the Federation and the crew of the Scorpio have discovered that some precious gems known as Feldon crystals are the potential source of an unlimited supply of energy. In fact, the Federation has invested millions upon millions of credits in trying to mine the gemstones.

One of the planets where the crystals have been found is Mecron, where mining is controlled by Belkov, a games player of great skill. He has set up and modified his own computer, Gambit, to play games with him continuously. The same computer also operates as a defence mechanism; however, defence and games are played in the same way and so defence mechanisms become games.

Belkov is reputed to have sent up an Orbiter full of Feldon crystals which he has mined and not released to the Federation, presumably for his own financial gain. For this reason, Servalan, under the name Commissioner Sleer, has arrived on the planet to find out why none of Belkov's original estimates of the amount of Feldon crystals that could be mined have in fact been reached.

Avon teams up with a Federation geologist who is also interested in double-crossing the Federation over the crystals, but before ·Avon can take any action, the geologist goes to Belkov's Orbiter and attempts to remove some crystals. The Orbiter is primed to play a series of games – these defeat the geologist and send him back injured to the rendezvous point with Scorpio.

As Federation investigations continue, Belkov takes advantage of the fact that the crystals are of deep religious significance to the Mecronians by playing the natives off against the Federation whilst making plans for his own escape. He traps Tarrant and Dayna in an underground cavern.

When Vila is ordered by Avon to remove part of the computer so that they can understand how Belkov's defence mechanisms work, he overhears instructions from

Belkov to the computer to self-destruct. Vila uses this knowledge to win the computer's acceptance and thus is able to free his trapped colleagues and dismantle part of the computer without being injured.

The crew of Scorpio teleport to Belkov's Orbiter, leaving Dayna on guard on Scorpio. They play a series of games in order to gain entrance to the inner part of the Orbiter, only to learn that the final game involves focusing the Feldon crystals on a black hole and so destroying everything in the vicinity. The crew teleport back to Scorpio, and Avon uses a blast from the Feldon crystals to counteract the pull of the black hole. Belkov appears to escape as his computer self-destructs, leaving the crew of Scorpio without the crystals which they were hunting. Even the crystals of a necklace that Vila stole from the planet appear to be fakes.

# SERIES D  EPISODE 9
# SAND

The planet Virn has been the subject of a series of strange reports from Keller and a team of Federation researchers. All have been wiped out mysteriously after discovering a unique energy source within the planet.

Servalan decides to travel to the planet with Chasgow her pilot, Investigator Reeve and an assistant. Turbulence causes them to crash-land and they realise that they will have to walk to the base established many years previously. They set out, leaving Chasgow – and a sandslide suddenly covers him and the crashed ship. At nightfall the party camp out and the assistant is swallowed by the sand, leaving just Servalan and Reeve.

Scorpio has likewise reached Virn in search of the energy source, and Dayna and Tarrant teleport down. Reeve injures Dayna, and Tarrant, under the influence of a strange force, has her teleported back to Scorpio but refrains from going back himself. Apparently shaking off the mysterious malady, Tarrant sets off after Reeve. They meet up at the base and Reeye is killed. Servalan appears and 'congratulates' Tarrant on his marksmanship.

In low orbit, the Scorpio crew are experiencing problems: the electrical storm over Virn has knocked all equipment out, with even Orac suffering interference. Down below, sheltering, Tarrant and Servalan explore the base computer area, which they find surprisingly undamaged by the hostile influences they are experiencing. They find food and the body of Keller, still strangely warm, whilst outside the green sand builds up, trapping them. Servalan reveals that Keller was once her lover. ...

On the ship Vila falls dangerously ill – affected by the sand which was teleported back with Dayna. Avon decides to manufacture a rain storm to counter the sand, and this they spectacularly do. Tarrant now realises that the sand is alive and manipulating events. He concludes that the sand wanted to breed humans to provide itself with more cellular tissue – hence, it would destroy individual men but keep a man and woman alive. Thus Keller had been allowed to live until his wife removed the sand's reasons for maintaining him by killing herself.

The rain storm permits both Tarrant and Servalan to escape. Despite the fact that each had had a gun on different occasions during their spell on Virn, neither was quite able to kill the other.


# SERIES D EPISODE 10
# GOLD

Avon meets an old acquaintance, Keiller, who is now purser of the Space Princess, a pleasure ship travelling from Zerok to Earth. Keiller says that although the Space Princess does indeed carry passengers, its real job is to transport gold from Zerok. He says that heavily armed

93

ships regularly leave Zerok supposedly carrying gold, but they are merely a decoy for the only lightly armed Space Princess. He suggests that the gold could be stolen from the Space Princess, except for one problem: before it leaves Zerok, the gold is automically transmuted to a black substance and has to be transmuted back before it is of any value. Keiller suggests further that the transmutation plant on Zerok can be tampered with, and that he has the technical knowledge to do it. This would leave the gold in its normal state and thus allow it to be stolen.

With only Vila left on Scorpio, the crew are teleported to Zerok, where they kill the guards and enter the underground mine. However alarm bells are set off and contrary to the plan there is a second attack of guards. Keiller, Tarrant and Dayna get back to Scorpio, but Avon and Soolin are erroneously thought to be dead on the planet. Avon comes to the conclusion that they have been set up, not only by Keiller but by someone else. Keiller admits that he has been used by an outside agency, but claims that he does not know who it is.

Upon returning to the ship, Avon determines that they should go ahead with the theft, despite having found that Keiller's last appointment was on the Presidential staff. On board the Space Princess, Avon and Keiller get the black gold whilst Dayna, who is disguised as a passenger, fakes an illness which will require her to be transported back to Zerok for treatment. The Space Princess puts out a distress call which is answered by Vila on Scorpio, and he agrees to take the ill Dayna back to Zerok.

When Scorpio and the Space Princess link up, Avon, Tarrant and Dayna, with Keiller, take the black gold aboard. They agree a rendezvous on Beta 5, where Keiller is expected to hand over the gold. As Avon completes the deal, the buyer is revealed to be Servalan and Avon admits that he has suspected this all the time. The crew of the Scorpio escape with the money handed over by Servalan whilst Servalan shoots Keiller, who has completed his usefulness for her. However once they are back on Scorpio, Orac informs the crew that Zerok has now ceded to the Federation and has thus come under the control of the Federation banking system, which has reformed the Zerok currency to bring it in line with Federation requirements. Thus the Zerok currency in which they have been paid is worthless, whilst Servalan has complete access to the gold.

# SERIES D EPISODE 11
# ORBIT

The crew of Scorpio are approached by Egrorian, a famed scientist who has been missing for many years. He offers them the Tachyon Funnel, which can destroy anything at any distance, instantly. Egrorian seems to be suspicious of Avon and demands that his shuttle craft be used for the journey down to the planet Malodaar rather than the teleport. Avon agrees and takes Vila with him.

On Malodaar they finally meet the grotesque Egrorian and his associate, the ancient Pinder. When the former demands Orac in return for the weapon, Avon agrees and he and Vila return to Scorpio. Avon convinces the rest of the crew of the need to go along with Egrorian, as the Funnel is undoubtedly now pointing at them.

However, before they return to the planet Tarrant asks Orac for details of the two scientists' histories and discovers that Egrorian is a wanted megalomaniac who mysteriously escaped the Federation ten years before. Pinder, it seems, should be only twenty-eight years old. Avon, already suspicious that Servalan may be behind the deal, travels back to the surface with Vila prepared for trouble.

With Servalan watching from the wings, the exchange takes place and Avon and Vila prepare to return to Scorpio once more. Egrorian confirms that Pinder is really only twenty-eight and appears to be over seventy because of exposure to Hoffal's Radiation, a by-product of the interaction between neutrons and magnetic forces. This gives Avon a partial insight into the working of the Tachyon Funnel.

On board the shuttle, Avon reveals that he has double-crossed Egrorian by giving him a dummy Orac, whilst Egrorian tells Servalan that he has made it impossible for the shuttle to attain orbit. They plan their departure without Pinder, and Pinder overhears.

As Avon discovers the problem on board the shuttle, Tarrant on Scorpio realises that the teleport system is unable to cope with the task of retrieving Avon and Vila from such a rapidly moving object. It is necessary for the shuttle to lose weight, and so it is stripped of all extraneous matter but still remains overweight. Baffled, Avon asks what weighs enough to save the situation and Orac tells him: Vila.

After a brief pause Avon sets out to kill Vila, but Vila has overheard and is hiding. Whilst searching, Avon realises that the weight problem is due to a fragment of a neutron star placed in plastic and left on the ship. He manages to jettison it just in time, whilst Vila, terrified, remains in hiding.

Back on the planet a disgusted Servalan leaves the scientists to rot. As soon as she leaves, Pinder takes his revenge on Egrorian by flooding the rooms with Hoffal's Radiation and thus killing them both.

## SERIES D  EPISODE 12
## WARLORD

Avon is growing more and more desperate in his attempts to win a victory over Servalan and to stop the spread of the Federation through its use of the drug Pylene 50. Whilst he has an antitoxin to the drug, he does not possess any method of manufacturing it and distributing

*1.* The Liberator, built by The System, found drifting in space and used by Blake to wage war on the Federation.

*2. Above* Blake's original crew in Liberator before the arrival of Cally: *left to right* Vila, Gan, Blake, Jenna, Avon.

*3. Below* The survivors of Blake's 7 in Scorpio: *left to right* Vila, Tarrant, Dayna, Avon, Soolin.

*4. Above* Cally ambushes Blake in Series A, Episode 4. Blake later persuaded Cally to join his crew and she continued to fight the Federation until dying on Terminal.

*5. Below* Blake and Avon meet their first aliens, the Decimas – artificially created but now fighting for their own self-respect.

6. *Above* Servalan, as always followed by guards, in Series D, Episode 8.

7. *Below* Tarrant amidst the wreckage of Scorpio having successfully crash-landed on Gauda Prime.

8. *Above* Vila who, despite the gun, existed in a constant state of fear.

9. *Below* Peter Tuddenham with two of the characters he played – Orac (foreground) and Slave.

10. *Above* Scorpio, a planet hopper modified by Dorian and used by Avon and his crew throughout Series D.

11. *Below* Dayna, self-assured and ready to fight at any moment.

12. A rare shot of Vere Lorrimer, director and producer, surrounded by his cast: *left to right* Vila, Soolin, Vere Lorrimer, Dayna, Tarrant, Avon.

*13.* The final moments – Avon shoots Blake, Series D, Episode 13.

it on a wide scale. Therefore he takes the enormous risk of summoning the leaders of five of the most powerful anti-Federation planets to a Summit meeting. The aim is to unite these warring factions to produce and distribute the antidote to Pylene 50 in sufficient quantities to combat the advance of the Federation. The success of the Summit depends on the co-operation of the most powerful warlord, Zukan. Zukan promises Avon access to the necessary raw material, which he claims is being produced on Zondawl.

Zukan's men unload the processing equipment onto Xenon base, helped by Zukan's daughter, Zeeona, who is on the base against the express wishes of her father. Having discovered his daughter's whereabouts, Zukan orders Avon and Soolin to take her back to Zondawl with them. However after they leave the planet Zeeona teleports back in order to be with Tarrant, with whom she has fallen in love.

A few hours after Scorpio leaves for Zondawl, Zukan departs and it becomes evident that he has double-crossed Avon, planted bombs on Xenon base, and done a deal with Servalan. But Servalan has herself planted a bomb on Zukan's ship. Three events follow quickly: the bombs go off on Xenon base and a radioactive airborne virus is let loose; the bomb is discovered on Zukan's ship, and although Zukan's lieutenant is jettisoned with the bomb, the ship is severely disabled; and Soolin and Avon discover that they have been tricked.

Tarrant and Vila attempt to dig their way out of Xenon base but meet with little success, whilst Zukan puts out an emergency distress call to Avon, who is now travelling back with Soolin. He demands rescue in return for helping the people trapped on Xenon base to escape, but the distance between his ship and Scorpio is too great for Avon to rescue him and then travel to the base in time. Still Zukan refuses to give the necessary information without being rescued, despite being told that his daughter is on the base.

Avon works out a temporary solution to the problem, and Tarrant and the others teleport on board Scorpio. Zeeona then teleports back down in order to deactivate the source of the virus – she succeeds but is killed in the process. Orac too has been severely disabled during the explosions on the base.

## SERIES D EPISODE 13
## BLAKE

Having failed in his attempt to get Zukan and the other warlords to unite in combatting the advance of Servalan, Avon decides to look for someone else to lead the dissidents against the Federation. At the same time, he is aware that Zukan has almost certainly told Servalan of the whereabouts of Scorpio's base. The crew of Scorpio therefore abandon the base and destroy it.

Once they are in flight, Avon reveals that Orac has tracked Blake down to Gauda Prime, the frontier planet on which Soolin lived as a child. Having been an 'Open Planet' for some time, on which the rule of Law has been suspended, Gauda Prime is now attempting to re-instigate the law, and hence a group of bounty hunters are on the planet rounding up and killing the criminals who have previously been roaming free. Despite Vila's incredulity at the idea that Blake could have become a bounty hunter, hunting criminals for cash, Orac is adamant that he has found him. Avon is certain that Blake is the right person to unite the anti-Federation forces once again and Scorpio proceeds to the planet.

On Gauda Prime, Blake appears battered and scarred. He is seen to shoot another bounty hunter in the back. He then captures Arlen, a tough fighter, whom he takes back to camp.

Approaching the planet, Scorpio comes under attack and suffers serious damage. Everyone teleports except

Tarrant, who stays at the controls and attempts to land the ship. Vila, Dayna and Soolin make their way to shelter and are caught up by Avon with Orac. Tarrant crashes the ship and is rescued by Blake, who takes him back to headquarters where he is handed over to Deva, presumably for a large reward. However it appears that this is only a test to discover Tarrant's suitability for Blake's cause.

Unfortunately Tarrant escapes before he can learn of this. He meets up with Avon and the others as they are entering the headquarters, having followed Blake in a stolen Flyer. As Tarrant tells Avon that Blake has betrayed them all, Blake appears and claims that he has been waiting on the planet for Avon to come. Avon is clearly unsure of the truth, and tells Blake to stand still. Despite this warning Blake continues to walk towards Avon, who shoots him.

Arlen reveals herself to be a Federation officer and is quickly knocked out by Vila, who then falls to the floor as a shot is heard. Federation guards appear and, in a brief shoot-out, Tarrant, Dayna and Soolin drop to the floor as time itself appears to slow down and the gun fire seems to echo endlessly. Avon has remained still throughout and no shots appear to be directed at him. As the dust settles and with no Federation guard moving against him he raises his gun, stands astride Blake and smiles. . . .

# In their own Words

## AVON AND BLAKE

It was not just Blake personally that Avon disliked – as he once said, 'I could never stand heroes,' and to him Blake was the personification of the fanaticism that lay behind all idealism. And it was this that made Blake a source of constant irritation to him: 'Blake is an idealist. He cannot afford to think. . . . I want to be free of *him*'.

Despite their antagonism, Blake was surprisingly complimentary to Avon at the final moment on Liberator: 'For what it is worth I have always trusted you, from the very beginning.' After Avon was left in charge, Blake still remained a subject for sarcasm. Once Vila said to him, 'Blake would've been proud of you, you know,' and Avon's reply came back, 'I know, but then he never was very bright'.

Avon was nothing if not prophetic. Speaking to Blake he said: 'Sooner or later, I will have my chance'. He was always certain that he would remain with Liberator longer than Blake: 'There will come a time when *he* won't be making the decisions'. And although he may not have been fully aware of it, his statement – 'Death is something that he and I faced together on a number of occasions. I always thought that his death and mine might be linked in some way' – takes on an eerie quality in retrospect.

So at the end it was Blake who had the final words,

spoken to his old enemy as he died: 'Avon, I was waiting for you ... Avon. ...' But if, after all that had gone before, he was genuinely waiting, this was not to be known.

## AVON IN HIS OWN WORDS

Avon's philosophy was clear. To Travis he said, 'I have no objection to shooting you in the back', which seems to leave little room for debate.

He had loved, and been betrayed, which deeply affected him, as when he remarked, 'Regret is part of being alive'. But if nothing else he was certainly self-sufficient: 'I don't take anything on trust'.

Despite everything he felt no friendship for the crew of Liberator, saying before leaving for Terminal, 'I don't need any of you. I needed the Liberator to bring me here, so I had no choice but to bring you along, but this is as far as you go. I don't want you with me, I don't want you following me. Understand this, anyone who does follow me, I'll kill them.' And just to make the point he added, 'Sentiment breeds weakness, let it get hold of you and you are dead.'

But there was more. He once said: 'I don't like an unsolved mystery,' and that led him into journeys which were never guided by self-interest.

Yet on the role of emotion he never wavered: 'I have never understood why it is necessary to become irrational in order to prove that you care, or why it should be necessary to prove it at all.'

His ability to remove emotion and analyse logically resulted in Dayna saying, as Jenna had said long before: 'Don't you ever get bored always being right?' and his reply was as might be expected, 'Only with you always being wrong.'

His relationship with Servalan became more and more

complex as time wore on. Despite everything, he recognised her single-minded drive for power at any cost as a form of strength and a rejection of emotion which he could, in some ways, admire. 'It's a great pity you and I have always been on opposite sides, Servalan,' he once said.

But finally on Gauda Prime he reflected a thought of Blake's which might well also have been in Servalan's mind more than once: 'In the end winning is the only safety.'

## VILA IN HIS OWN WORDS

Vila was not only a coward – he was humorous too, and even when terrified could still make a joke. 'Leave me a torch, I like to see what I'm scared of,' he said on being thrown into a dark dungeon. Action, he knew, meant trouble: 'No to whatever it was.' But his way with words could get him in trouble, as when he said to Bayban, 'You have a reputation for mayhem which is second to none. I have been an admirer of yours for, well, as long as I can remember. Well, maybe not that long, I mean you are not that old are you? But then again, you did start very young didn't you – I think I feel sick.'

Vila had one big chance of escape from Avon and Blake – with Kerril, the girl he loved. But something held him back: 'A thief isn't what I am, it's who I am.' On leaving Kerril, he said, 'I think I have just made the biggest mistake of my life,' and Orac couldn't resist saying, 'It is unlikely. I would predict there are far greater mistakes waiting to be made by someone with your obvious talent for it.'

And so it was back to resigned comments like, 'I don't believe in suicide, it stunts your growth,' and the usual one-liners: 'I have just worked out a completely new strategy, it's called running away,' and 'I plan to live for ever, or die trying,' or in desperation, 'The Himalayas are quite tall at this time of year.' Still he never forgot his trade: 'There isn't a lock I can't open – if I'm scared enough.'

He was no more flattering in his assessment of other people's characters than he was of his own. Of Dorian he said, 'There is something very suspicious about a man who keeps his booze under lock and key.' Whilst of Tarrant he said, 'He has about as much idea of subtlety as a Targaan Warg Strangler.' Of Avon he said, 'There isn't a volcano alive that would dare to swallow Avon,' and to the universe in general, 'Stealing is quicker.'

However, with Avon he had a strange understanding that came from the mutual respect each had for the other's talents: 'This is stupid' (Vila). 'When did that ever stop us?' (Avon). But with Avon he rarely got the last word: 'I've got this shocking pain right behind the eyes' (Vila). 'Have you considered amputation?' (Avon).


## QUOTATIONS – OTHER SOURCES

Nothing summed up the Federation better than its own official phrase: 'From strength to unity,' and as for its Supreme Commander, 'She has all the sensitive delicacy of plasma bolt' (said by Senator Bercol).

This was backed up by Servalan's own sayings: 'While there's life there's threat,' and 'Hope is very dangerous'.

Generally speaking, the Federation officers and executives rarely managed to make impressive use of language. For example, Travis's most memorable words were virtually his last, spoken as he deactivated the defence zone around Star One which let in the alien invasion: 'The final act'. He was then shot by Blake and Avon.

On board Liberator and Scorpio however, things were more lively. Orac, for example, was rarely short of an opinion: 'I have noticed that the occupants of this space craft have a lamentable lack of interest in the more fascinating aspects of the Universe.' And on another occasion, 'I am not interested in trying to compensate for your amazing lack of observation.' In his own defence he postulated that 'A statement of fact cannot be insolent.'

Of the other crew members, only Cally came close to rivalling Avon and Vila in their endless stream of sayings and rebuffs, and her statements often came from her own people's history: 'There is a saying among my people. A man who trusts can never be betrayed, only mistaken,' which brought the inevitable reply from Avon that 'Life expectancy must be fairly short among your people.' Perhaps her toughest and most memorable line was her first on meeting Blake, expressing the horror that must pursue all telepaths: 'May you die alone and silent.'

# The Index

This index contains references to all characters, places and events mentioned in the TV series.

It was the convention during the period spanned by 'Blake's 7' for a person to use only one name, a name which might be the given name or a surname. Hence everybody knew Avon by his surname but Vila by his given name. In the index the commonly used name of each character determines its alphabetical position. Hence Vila Restal is under 'V' whilst Roj Blake is under 'B'. The spelling adopted is that given in the initial BBC documentation for each programme. From time to time spellings were changed in the subsequent scripts, the *Radio Times* entries and the three novels. These variations have been ignored.

The programmes never make clear how many years in the future the events of 'Blake's 7' take place. However it is suggested that the first inter-stellar ships left Earth 700 years before Blake. Since we are clearly at least 100 years away from any development of a stellar drive, we may consider Blake to be between 800 and 1,000 years in the future. The relatively short space of time spent in space (700 years) explains the thinness of the populations on most planets.

The series is situated within the galaxy known to us as the Milky Way. Our galaxy contains around $10^{11}$ stars (that means 10 with 11 noughts on the end) and perhaps five times as many planets. Its radius is 81,500 light years (1 ly $= 5.88 \times 10^{12}$ miles). The Earth is 32,600 ly from the centre. The average distance between the stars is about 3 ly, although at the centre of the galaxy it may be as low as 0.1 ly. Andromeda Galaxy (the source of the invasion) is 2,185,000 ly away.

**ABSORPTION** – Method by which the Core of Ultraworld grew. It absorbed species that were encountered by the Ultra after their personality profiles had been wiped clean through Transference.

**ADMINISTRATION** – Section of the Federation that controlled Earth.

**ADRENALIN AND SOMA** – Intoxicating drink: see Soma.

**AGRAVO** – Planet completely mined by the Federation. The planet was destroyed by a series of explosions caused by Feldon crystals which killed thousands of people.

**ALBIAN** – Planet with a breathable atmosphere and temperate equatorial weather regions, but uninhabitable at the poles. Population approximately 6 million. They joined the Federation only after a long period of resistance.

**A-LINE PULSE CODE** – Used by Federation for top security messages.

**ALPHA GRADE** – Grading used on Earth for a highly privileged intellectual group of which Blake was a member.

**ALPHA 3** – Belkov's ship used in his plan to escape from the planet Mecron.

**ALPHA 7/5** – An organic member of the cactus family that was the main constituent of the drug Shadow. The cactus (also known as Moon Disc) was prized for its partial telepathy.

**ALTA 1** – Along with Alta 2, recaptured the Liberator on behalf of the System. They were the voice and arms of the System.

**ALTERN 5** – Federation planet, source of Selsium Ore.

**AMAGONS** – Primarily pirates, but also involved in smuggling and various other acts of piracy. Once captured the Liberator.

**ANDROIDS** – Sophisticated robot-like creatures highly developed by the Federation. Among the most sophisticated was that developed by Muller, a pupil of Ensor. His android had all the power of Orac plus a circuit influencer and mobility. Its nearest rivals were the android version of Avalon created by Federation scientists and Vinni the gunfighter who became Champion of Vandor.

**ANDROMEDA** – Nearest large spiral galaxy to our own, known astronomically as M31 or NGC224. It was the source of the invasion fleet in the Intergalactic War.

**ANDROMEDANS** – Multicoloured jellyfish-like creatures, measuring about 6 feet across and with highly advanced technological ability.

**ANTI-MATTER MINE FIELD** – Built by the Federation to keep out any threat from Andromeda. It acted as both an alarm system and minefield, and existed between Star One and Andromeda.

**AQUATAR** – Project on which both Avon and Blake worked to develop an alloy which would allow the reduction and transmission of matter as pure energy. The teleport bracelets on the Liberator were based on the same concept.

**ARBITER** – Highest human authority within a Federation Court.

**ARCO** – One of the prisoners transported on the ship London.

**ARDUS** – Ex-officer of Federation Central Intelligence Control. Blinded by a radiation flare on Bucol 2, he was killed at Servalan's command.

**ARISTO** – Planet on which Ensor built and maintained Orac. Nine-tenths of Aristo was covered by water, the land masses were arid, the oceans highly acidic. There had been a number of cities built by earlier civilisations but the rising of the water had covered almost all of these. Life was slowly beginning to evolve in the oceans by the time of Blake's visit.

**ARLE** – Rebel soldier who worked for Kasabi.

**ARLEN** – Federation officer, captured by Blake on Gauda Prime and recruited to his cause in the belief she was an outlaw.

**ARTIX** – Junior officer on the space ship transporting Blake to Cygnus Alpha.

**A S HILL** – Headquarters of the Hommiks.

**ASYMMETRIC THRUST COMPUTER** – Part of the Liberator control system under the control of Zen.

**ASTEROID PK118** – Tiny planetary body, diameter 0.102 spacials. The asteroid was removed from planetary orbit so that it could be mined more easily, mining being completed three years before the visit of the Liberator crew. Life support was installed by the mining company.

**ASTRID** – Federation Colonel who was kept in suspended animation by Grose after he took over his command on Sardos.

**ATLAN** – Leader of the Space Rats, although not a Space Rat himself.

**ATLAY** – Location of the annual meeting of all governors of the Federation.

**ATOMIC WAR** – Major war affecting much of the galaxy, occurring several hundred years before Blake's birth. It was in the aftermath of this war that the Federation arose.

**AURON** – Home planet of Cally. The inhabitants had telepathic powers and prized their isolation. Cally and others were outlawed for becoming involved in outside affairs. Servalan launched an alien pathogen onto Auron and wiped out the entire population. However some gene banks were saved and transferred to a new planet.

**AURONAR** – Outlawed members of Cally's people who used telepathic power to force her to bring the

Liberator to their planet. They specialised in tissue regeneration and cleaned up an injury on Blake's arm within seconds.

**AUROS** – Planet on which Travis massacred innocent civilians, with the result that he was suspended from duty.

**AVALON** – Federation resistance leader who started resistance movements on some half a dozen planets.

**AVERSION THERAPY** – Used by Servalan on Dayna: it produced a rapid conditioned response of first hatred, then deep love.

**AVON** – Native of Earth, one of the leading electronics and computer experts of the age, full name Kerr Avon. He attempted to embezzle 500 million credits from the Federation banking cartel, and upon the failure of the attempt was sent to a penal colony, en route for which he met Blake. Avon was certainly not above blackmail, shooting someone in the back, or even disposing of Vila if that was required for his own survival. His code of logic and practical necessity was heightened by the discovery that his girlfriend had betrayed him in his embezzlement attempt. His ambivalent attitude to Blake meant that he disliked him whilst twice being drawn back to him. Despite Avon's dislike of Vila's cowardice, he was known to admit that the inherent suspicion Vila displayed frequently made him 'right'. Towards the end Avon was clearly developing a form of paranoia due to the constant strain of living on the edge of death.

**A X RIDGE** – Site of the final battle between the Seska and the Hommiks on Xenon.

**B19 CRUISERS** – Federation Search Ships.

**BALON** – Comrade of Sula on Earth.

**BARLEE** – Space ship on which Docholli travelled to Freedom City. After an on-board explosion Docholli performed emergency surgery on Travis.

**BARR** – Hi Tech bounty hunter on Chenga.

**BARTOLOMEW** – Anna Grant/Sula. Federation

Central Security's top agent who, acting as Avon's girlfriend Anna, betrayed him completely.

**BASE COMMANDER** – Rank within the Federation.

**BATTLE COMPUTERS** – Section of the computing system on Liberator controlled by Zen which automatically computed the best manoeuvres for the ship when attacking or when under attack. The battle computers suffered from the disadvantage of having to be put on line via an instruction from one of the crew, thus wasting valuable seconds during a surprise attack.

**BAX** – Doctor on Fosforon.

**BAYBAN** – Space pirate and the Federation's most wanted criminal, variously known as Bayban the Berserker and Bayban the Butcher.

**BEARING** – Similar to a compass position, used on the Liberator.

**BEK** – Companion of Hanna involved in the fight against the Terra Nostra.

**BELHANGRIA UNIVERSITY** – Centre of mathematical excellence attended by Egrorian.

**BELKOV** – Highly skilled games player and Federation mining agent on Meeron.

**DR BELLFRIAR** – Eminent scientist on Fosforon.

**BENOS** – Pirate and slave seller on Domo.

**BERCOL** – Senator and Head of the Information Bureau. Ex officio member of the High Council.

**BERG** – Soldier working for Kasabi. Killed with Arle.

**BERSHAR** – Son of Hower, the first citizen of Obsidian. He betrayed his planet to Servalan.

**BETAFARL** – Ruled by Zukan, the planet had perpetual day, presumably because it revolved around a binary star system.

**BETA FIVE** – Federation Planet in the Ark Rough Bennett Complex in a group of stars abandoned by the Federation.

**BETA REGION** – Region of space in which Asteroid PK118 was situated.

**THE BIG WHEEL** – Largest casino on Freedom City. The Big Wheel was run by a computer which fixed the odds at 5% in favour of the house.

**BLACK HOLE** – Dense object with such a high gravity that not even light can escape from its pull.

**ROJ BLAKE** – Native of Earth. An Alpha Grade engineer, he became leader of the Freedom Party and saw most of his friends murdered by Travis. After brainwashing he renounced his old beliefs at his trial. However after breaking through the mind blocks he was tried again and found guilty of various crimes against young children. After his escape from custody he used Liberator to continue his fight against the Federation, risking his own life and sometimes the lives of others for the cause. He was seriously injured by Travis on Star One but was reported uninjured by Zen after the Intergalactic War. He finally appeared on Gauda Prime, where he was killed by Avon. At least two Blake clones were made, and one remained alive with a slave girl on an unnamed planet after the Imipak affair.

**BLIND SUN** – Star without any planetary system.

**BLISTER FORCE WALL** – Small force wall surrounding only one part of a ship.

**BOMBER** – Underling of Atlan on Caspar.

**BOORVA** – Planetary leader brought into an anti-Federation alliance with Zukan, Chalsa, Lod and Mida by Avon.

**BORDER SYSTEMS** – Phrase used by Avon to describe those planets about to fall to Federation control through the use of Pylene 50.

**BORR** – Intelligence commander who worked in Federation Central Intelligence Control.

**BOUNTY HUNTER** – Hunter of criminals and outlaws for cash. Used by the government of Gauda Prime to try to clean up the planet before restoration of Federation law.

**BUCOL 2** – Planet used by the Federation as a base for a

genetic engineering research programme to combat the effects of radiation.

**BUREAU** – Abbreviated name for Federation Central Intelligence Control.

**CA 1 & 2** – Senior officials on Auron.

**CALCOS** – Federation penal colony planet.

**CALIPHERON** – Planet to which the Liberator was to take its crew in the event that Avon failed to return from Terminal.

**CALIPH OF CRANDOR** – Second-in-command to Thaarn.

**CALLISTO** – Large asteroid in the solar system used by smugglers as a base.

**CALLY** – Native of Auron who was exiled because of her involvement in the fight against the Federation. She met Blake whilst planning a solo attack on Saurian Major. Despite the fact that the Auron do not normally have paranormal abilities beyond telepathy, her long association with the crew of Liberator led her to develop abilities of mind-reading, precognition and telekinesis. She remained with Liberator in order to fight the Federation, and died on Terminal following the explosion set by Servalan.

**CANCER** – Professional killer, also known as Piri.

**CARNELL** – Psycho-strategist who worked for Servalan in order to get Imipak.

**CARTHANOS** – Frontier world on which climate control went wrong before the main attack on Star One.

**CASPAR** – Earth-type planet in Sector 5.

**CATO** – Assistant to Gun-sar on Xenon. Discovered an ancient computer complex which had been over-looked when it was decided, after the Xenon war, that all technology should be swept aside. He had learned it and was maintaining the city, and its position of power, through it.

**CAUDER** – Resistance leader on Albian.

**C E C** – Central Educational Complex, a major training establishment run by the Federation for the training of rulers of planets which were under Federation influence.

**CENTERO** – Planet under Federation control which housed the major security installation. It was from this planet that Blake attempted to steal a message decoder.

**CENTRAL RECORD FILE 15/9/834** – File on Egrorian held in Federation Central Records.

**CEPHLON** – Planet with breathable atmosphere of high oxygen content but with an unacceptably high radiation level (the result of a series of wars on the planet). After the war the inhabitants reverted to barbarism.

**CEVEDIC** – Agent of Krantor who captured Travis and took him to Servalan in Freedom City. Eventually killed by Travis.

**CF1** – Reform institution with which Vila was placed as a boy. He led the escape bid by the inmates.

**CHAIRMAN** – Leader of the Terra Nostra.

**CHALSA** – Planetary leader brought into an alliance with Zukan, Boorva, Lod and Mida by Avon.

**CHARL OF THE TENTS OF GOTH** – King of the planet Goth.

**CHASGOW** — Servalan's pilot on the journey to Virn.

**CHEL** – Leader of the Sarrans.

**CHENEY** – Subcommander with the Federation on an uninhabited planet guarding President Sarkoff.

**CHENGA** – Neutral planet settled 200 years before the Intergalactic War. It operated the hospital ship that picked up Cally and Servalan.

**CHENIE** – Barmaid on Freedom City. She worked in the bar that was frequented by Docholli.

**CHESIL** – Inhabitant of Sardos.

**CHESKU** – Federation High Councillor and advisor to Servalan. Married to Sula, who killed him.

**CHEVNER** – Freedom Fighter working with Avalon. He was killed by the android Avalon after escaping from the Federation forces with Blake onto Liberator.

**CITY AT THE EDGE OF THE WORLD** – Ancient city on the planet Keezarn.

**CIVIL ADMINISTRATION SHIP LONDON** – The ship which transported Blake et al to Cygnus Alpha.

**CLASS-GRADING** – All Federation citizens were graded Alpha to Delta. Blake was Alpha, Vila was Delta.

**CLIP-GUN** – Developed by Dorian for use on Scorpio. Made of Argentium, recoil-less and able to fire under water. Designed to fire a variety of projectiles, it had a guidesight mounted on top and laser guiding towards the target. Each clip fired a different projectile, each being colour coded. The black clip fired plasma bolts.

**CLONE-BLAKE** – Created by Fen on Servalan's command. The clone survived with Rashel on an uninhabited planet.

**CLONING** – Controlled by the Clonemasters, who could create life in any form but who had very strong moral principles and guarded their secrets well. Cloning was also developed by Clinician Franton on Auron.

**COMBAT GROUNDS** – Set of different environments maintained by the Teal-Vandor Convention within a giant computer. The scene of the fight to the death between the champions of Teal and Vandor.

**CONTROL** – Main computer complex set up by the Federation on Earth to monitor all political, military and other sensitive activity throughout their empire. It was initiated two centuries before, when the Federation started its programme of expansion.

**CONTROLLED BEAMING** – Method of artificial telepathic transmission developed on Auron.

**CORE** – Centre of Ultraworld, its living heart and brain. It was the object of the Ultra to increase the Core and to protect it at all times. The Core existed to expand, and only through expansion could it actually live.

**COSER** – Beta Class weapons technician who invented and then stole Imipak. He was killed by Servalan using his own invention.

**COUNCIL OF THE FEDERATION** – Equivalent to an unelected parliament through which the President ruled. Technically the Supreme Commander of the armed forces was answerable to the Council. However, political intrigue and in-fighting meant that the Councillors and Supreme Commander invariably held each other in mistrust and, where possible, at a distance.

**COUNCIL OF SURVIVORS** – Group of rulers on the planet Xenon who decided that the Hommiks should start their civilisation again from scratch after the wars which reduced them to barbarism.

**CRANDOR** – Artificial planet created by Thaarn and destroyed by Groff.

**CRIMINO THERAPY** – Method of brainwashing employed by the Federation on criminal and political deviants. The method involved the use of trigger signals for hypnotic states which conditioned convicted offenders for memory revision. The signal was then used to keep the criminal under control.

**CRIMOS** – Abbreviated word meaning criminal psychopaths. Crimos had high IQs but enjoyed inflicting pain. They were used by Travis after he became a Federation outlaw.

**CRYOGENIC CAPSULE** – Capsule in which an individual's life could be suspended by freezing in order to survive long journeys in space.

**THE CURSE OF CYGNUS** – Illness which was supposed to keep people on the planet Cygnus Alpha. The disease was carried in the atmosphere.

**CYGNUS ALPHA** – Federation prison planet to which Blake and the others were sent in the ship London.

**CYGNUS XL** – Black hole in the galaxy, one of the stars that Gambit recognised as completing a games sequence.

**DAINER** – One of the guards on the space ship transporting Blake to Cygnus Alpha. It was Dainer whom Vila tricked by some simple subterfuge so that Blake's entry onto the ship's walkway would be unnoticed.

**DARKLING ZONE** – Popular name of 61 Cygni.

**DARLON IV** – Frontier world which, according to some reports, was the home planet of Soolin on which her parents were murdered. However she stated that this happened on Gauda Prime.

**DAYNA MELLANBY** – Daughter of Hal Mellanby, born on Earth and then taken back to Sarran after her father's revolutionary group had fallen. Dayna developed an early interest in weapons technology. She rescued Avon from the warriors on Sarran and, after her father's death, returned to Liberator with Avon. She apparently died on Gauda Prime.

**KARL DECCA** – One of the children supposed to have been molested by Blake, which alleged act resulted in his second trial.

**DECIMAS** – Small animal-like machines created by the Auronar. Decimas appeared to be quite harmless but were cruelly treated by the Auronar. Early generations showed no aggressive tendencies, but these were later manifested to a significant degree.

**DEEP SPACE VEHICLE 2** – The System's name for Liberator.

**DEETA TARRANT** – Brother of Del. First Champion of the United Planets of Teal, killed by the android Vinni.

**DEL 10** – Planet mentioned by Vila as paradise which the crew of Liberator should visit. Reputed to be the galaxy's biggest source of atmospheric Beta Particles.

**DELTA 714** – Blind star on the edge of Sector 6, the region in which the Liberator was eventually destroyed.

**DELTA GRADE** – Lowest grading on Earth. Vila was a Delta Service Grade.

**DERAL** – Federation captain serving under Servalan.

**DESTINY** – Planet colonised 100 years before Blake took the Liberator, home of Dr Kendall. It was outside the Federation, and was based on an agricultural economy.

**DETECTOR RANGE** – The distance at which one space ship can detect the presence of another in open space.

**DETECTOR SHIELD** – Masking device used on certain Federation ships from time to time, invented by Avon. The Liberator once had a Detector Shield, but it was put out of operation and stayed out for a prolonged time due to lack of spare parts. Avon suggested that he was at one time hoping to sell the Federation the idea of the Detector Shield, only to discover that they had already invented it themselves.

**DEVA** – Controller on Gauda Prime working with Blake.

**DIAGNOSTIC ANALYSER** – Part of the standard medical kit on board the Liberator, used to find out exactly what was wrong with people taken ill.

**DISINTRESTRA** – Planet capable of supporting carbon-based life forms, passed by the Liberator on the way to Terminal.

**DISORIENTER** – Federation device used on Horizon to disorientate subjects in order to make them reveal information. It was used on Blake and Jenna.

**DOCHOLLI** – Federation cyber-surgeon, reputed to be the only man knowing the whereabouts of Star One. Docholli operated on the technicians who built Star One in order to remove its location from their memories.

**DOMO** – Hostile planet near the edge of the Sixth Quadrant, used by pirates.

**DORAN** – Passenger on the transporter to which Tarrant and Vila were teleported while travelling in the vicinity of the planet Sardos. Doran had just completed a fifteen-year prison term on the penal colony Calcos when he met Vila.

**DORIAN** – 'Rescued' the survivors of Liberator after it had been destroyed on Terminal. When asked, he described himself as a salvage operator. During his long life, Dorian had become an expert on weaponry system design, computers and computer repairs – he was able to repair the damaged Orac – and apparently numerous other fields. He also claimed to have met Ensor, the designer of Orac. Dorian was around 200-years-old when the survivors of the Liberator first met him.

**DORTMUNN** – Flight Engineer on board the Galaxy Class ship Ortega.

**DREAM HEAD** – An addict of the drug Shadow.

**DRUGS** – The Liberator kept a wide range of drugs, much to the delight of Vila. Among the many that pleased him was a mixture prepared by Cally – one third Adrenalin, two thirds Soma. See also Shadow, Soma, Exobriddan, and Relaxant.

**DURKIM** – Associate of Servalan.

**DYNAMIC FLUX MATHS** – Studied by Tarrant. Thaarn also used it in his calculations to increase the gravity generator.

**DYNAMON** – Crystals used on Xenon as rare and precious jewels worn by women.

**EARTH** – Base of the Terran Federation and home planet of all the crew of Scorpio and Liberator except Gan, Cally and Soolin. The inhabitants were kept inside giant domes, and attempts to go outside were considered serious offences. The water and air supplies within the domes were drugged in order to ensure the passive obedience of the populace. Space travellers had set out some 700 years before Blake to explore the galaxy, but Earth remained the most populated planet in the Federation.

**ECLIPSE PATTERN** – Federation method of attack using three spaceships to attack one hostile ship. Only two ships were seen at any one time, one being in the shadow of the other, and the third ship remained totally hidden at all times.

**EGRORIAN** – Brilliant but megalomaniacal scientist. When his attempt to take over the Federation failed, he retreated with Servalan's help to Malodaar, where he developed the Tachyon Funnel.

**EGRORIAN THEORY OF PARALLEL MATTER** – Theoretical base of the Tachyon Funnel, of such a complex nature that few in the galaxy could follow it.

**ELEVENTH SECTOR** – Location of Star One, an otherwise deserted region of space between our galaxy and Andromeda.

**ENERGY MASS TRANSMUTER** – Machine which analysed the molecular structure of any particular object and then replicated it.

**ENFORCER** – Underling of Largo who killed his superior in order to take his place and his wealth.

**ENSOR** – Developer of the Tarriel Cell, which all computers on the known planets contained. He also developed a number of new concepts in computer technology and taught some brilliant students, including Muller, before disappearing to Aristo in order to continue his work unhampered. His final achievement was the development of Orac. His son died on board Liberator whilst attempting to force Blake to take the ship to Aristo.

**EPHERON** – Planet of the star Loritol and last known location of Blake after the Intergalactic War until his unexpected appearance on Gauda Prime.

119

**EPINAARL** – Planet populated by non-humanoids who were intelligent but very hostile to all humanoid life forms.

**ESCAPE VELOCITY** – Speed which a space ship has to obtain in order to leave a planet and not be drawn back by its gravity.

**ESCON** – Base Commander working under Travis.

**EXOBRIDDAN** – Highly addictive drug. Dayna pretended to be suffering from Exobriddan addiction whilst on the Space Princess.

**EXTRA RANGE DETECTORS** – Detectors on board the Liberator which, although exceptionally useful for spotting Federation pursuit ships at long distances, put enormous strain on the energy banks and so were rarely if ever used.

**FARREN** – Administrative assistant on XK72.

**FATIGUE SHOCK** – State of stress due to too many calls on physical and mental reserves. The crew of the Liberator were seen to be suffering from it as early as Series B Episode 4, and this may be the ultimate explanation for Avon's paranoia and eventual seeming betrayal of the crew in the final episode.

**FEDERATION** – Abbreviated name for the Terran Federation. A fascist dictatorship set up in the aftermath of the galaxy-wide Atomic Wars, it controlled thousands of planets (divided into the Inner and Outer Worlds) and was governed by the President and the High Council. An uneasy balance existed between the President and the military wing, Space Command, until Supreme Commander Servalan overthrew the President and set up a military dictatorship. During Servalan's absence on Terminal however, she was in turn overthrown and her supporters killed. There were constant attempts by Federation planets to rebel, but supression was rigorously enforced. The Federation's greatest

120

problem was a surfeit of human beings below the privileged Alpha Class. Where possible (as on Earth), these people were kept docile through drugs in their air and water supplies. Personal freedom was non-existent under the Federation, and all religions banned. All citizens were required to register their residence and could not move without re-registering. Private transport was prohibited and interplanetary movement was forbidden without a permit. Worlds which were settled by people from Earth but were still outside the Federation were known as the Outer Planets. Once absorbed into the Federation, they became part of the Outer Worlds.

**FEDERATION CENTRAL CONTROL** – Complex housing the central data banks in which records of all criminals, suspected criminals, terrorists and dissenters within the Federation were kept.

**FEDERATION CIVIL LIST** – List of Federation supporters who were not in the armed forces but could be called upon to take positions of civil leadership when required.

**FEDERATION WEAPONS DEVELOPMENT BASE** – A 'Triple A' security base.

**FELDON CRYSTALS** – Precious stones which could be used as a great power source. Feldon was the hardest known substance in the universe, and hence the most valuable. It was particularly rare, and was prized as a precious stone until industrial and commercial uses were discovered. Feldon concentrated energy in a way that was infinitely more efficient than a burning glass. It might eventually have turned out to be a source of unlimited energy and could have been used to create, among other things, series of multiple traction beams. Belkov suggested that he would use his Orbiter and the moon of Mecron to do this in order to keep Scorpio in position if the crew refused to help him.

**FEN** – Clonemaster who dealt with Servalan in making the Clone Blake.

**FINN** – Lieutenant to Zukan. He aided Zukan in the partial destruction of Xenon base, but was later killed by a bomb which Zukan forced him to dismantle.

**FLUID IN SPACE** – An apparent anomaly encountered by the Liberator en route for Terminal. It caused the eventual destruction of the ship.

**FORBIDDEN ZONE** – Zone around the Control Centre on Earth.

**FORBUS** – Inventor of Pylene 50. Commissioner Sleer made Forbus work to produce the drug although he had no desire to do so, knowing to what use it was put.

**FORCE FIELD** – All force fields appear and feel solid. However, they are obviously not. Force fields return all energy put into them and thus cannot be destroyed simply by burning or lasers.

**FORCE WALL** – Defence mechanism on Liberator which acted as a force shield against plasma bolts and other missiles. It was possible to counter-attack through the force wall of Liberator, but it involved maximum deflection being instigated first, set to overlock rather than interlap. The force wall on Liberator took up a large amount of power, and it was impossible to operate concurrently with the main drive for a long period of time because of the resultant energy drain. This was always a difficulty when encountering various obstacles such as meteor showers.

**FORRESS** – Section Leader guarding Residence 1 on Earth.

**FOSFORON** – Planet with a radio link base. All life was eradicated by an alien virus.

**BRAD FOSTER** – Friend of Blake's in the Freedom Party.

**FRANTON** – Auron woman in charge of the Replication Programme; daughter of the inventor of the

Replication Plant.

**CLINICIAN FRANTON** – Inventor of cloning on Auron, killed during the Intergalactic War.

**FREEDOM CITY** – Frontier town on a planet outside the Federation to which Docholli escaped.

**FREEDOM PARTY** – Party to which Blake belonged before his initial trial and rehabilitation by the Federation. Blake renounced the Freedom Party after having been indoctrinated by the Federation.

**GALACTIC MONOPOLY** – One of the games played on Liberator and much enjoyed by Orac.

**GALAXY** – All of the episodes of 'Blake's 7' occur within our own galactic system, commonly known today as the Milky Way. The main reference to beings from another galaxy occurs in the Intergalactic War at the end of Series B Episode 13. However, in Series A Episode 8, Travis suggests that he was now pursuing Blake in another galaxy. This would appear to be in direct contradiction of comments made in Series B Episode 13, in which it is clearly suggested that travel between the island galaxies is beyond even the power of the Liberator. Thus it seems reasonable to assume that Travis meant to say that Blake had wandered into a remote part of our own galaxy.

**GALAXY CLASS CRUISERS** – Spaceships manufactured by the Outer Planets, not the Federation. The Mark IIIs went out of production fifty years before Blake took over the Liberator.

**GALT** – Deputy Commander with the Federation.

**GAMBIT** – Computer used by Belkov to play games. It was basically an Alpha Class 197 which had undergone major modifications, including the addition of circuits from the PPC Class machine. As a result of these changes it had managed to develop its own volition, and this it used to Belkov's ultimate disadvantage.

**GAMBRIL** – Junior Officer working under Dr Bellfriar on Fosforon.

**GAMES** – The greatest games player encountered by the crew of Liberator and later Scorpio was Belkov. Among his games was a shooting match in which the participant was pitted against a computer projection of him or herself. The computer was programmed to match the skill and ability of the participant for the first two shots, but on the third shot exceeded it. Thus the computer always won and the participant always died at his or her 'own' hand. See also Galactic Monopoly.

**GAN** – Native of Zephron. When he saw a Federation guard rape his girlfriend, Gan killed him, was certified insane and had a Limiter placed in his head to stop him killing again. Gan showed great courage and was always willing to use his great physical strength to help others. He also had a strong streak of common sense, although by his own admission he was not particularly bright. He died on Earth during the attempt to destroy Control – the first member of the '7' to be lost.

**GAUDA PRIME** – Frontier planet, commonly known as GP. Home of Soolin, where her parents were murdered. It was an agricultural world declared an open planet in order to speed up the mining of resources.

**GEDDEN** – Planet involved in the Intergalactic War which was supposedly the location of the death of Servalan during a rear-guard action.

**GEELA** – Genetically manipulated member of the Auronar. 'Sister' of Novara.

**GENETIC ENGINEERING** – Banned by the Federation but nevertheless undertaken by Auron exiles, both to create immortality in humans (Geela and Novara) and to develop a new form of life that would undertake menial tasks (Decimas). Also used by the Federation under Justin on Bucol 2 to develop creatures able to exist in high radiation areas without being contaminated.

**GERMAINIAN CIRCUITRY** – Circuitry from which Ultraworld was built.

**GERREN** – Academician, geologist and expert on mining techniques who was part of the survey team for the Feldon project. He teamed up with Avon in an attempt to get some personal profit from the Feldon project, but was seriously injured in attempting to beat Belkov's game computer.

**GESARUS** – Site of a major plague which killed millions.

**GESTALT** – Creature inhabiting the room in the depths of Dorian's stronghold on Xenon. The Gestalt contained all of the psychic wave patterns of Dorian, which had been absorbed in order to leave him free of any marks of the aging process, as well as the marks of his own experiences and corruptions. For this absorption process to work, the creature had been fed with the bodies of Dorian's original partner and others over the years. There was thus a similarity between Dorian's creature and the Core of Ultraworld. The word 'gestalt' is widely used in 20th-century psychology to mean an entity in which the whole is more than the sum of the parts.

**GINKA** – Federation Officer working under Servalan and Deral. He was resentful that Deral had been made a captain whilst he was not. After plotting against Deral he achieved his desired rank, but soon blundered and was killed by Servalan.

**GIROC** – The Keeper who, with Sinofar, controlled the Power, the remains of a race which destroyed itself after thousands of years of war on an unnamed planet.

**VEN GLYND** – Federation Arbiter General who prosecuted Blake at his trial for offences against children. Blake met Glynd for a second time on the asteroid PK118 after Glynd had defected from the Federation's cause and had developed the plan of installing Blake as the new Federation leader along-side Le Grand and Shivan.

**GOLA** – Tribal leader (Charl) on the planet Goth. Gola's wounds were once healed by the surgeon Lurgen.

**GOLD** – Remained a highly prized metal during the time of the Federation. Gold was mined out on virtually every planet except Zerok, where it was plentiful and mined in great quantities. Gold was still used as a standard currency in dealings with planets that had no computer link-ups.

**GOTH** – Planet to which Lurgen was reported to have travelled after escaping from the Federation following the building of Star One. Its surface had a wide range of toxic gases, including sulphur, thus forcing inhabitants to retreat below ground level.

**GOW** – Federation base for mind therapists.

**ANNA GRANT** – Girlfriend of Avon who, working under the name Bartolomew, betrayed him. She also used the name Sula and was married to High Councillor Chesku. Avon finally killed her on Earth.

**DEL GRANT** – Mercenary leader of the rebels on the planet Albian. Grant believed that Avon had deliberately left his sister Anna to die in order to escape the Federation and thus vowed to kill Avon. In fact it was Anna who betrayed Avon.

**GRAPHIC WRITING STICK** – Pencil.

**GRAVITATIONAL VORTEX** – Gravitational spiral which acted rather like a whirlpool. It was at the heart of the Prohibited Zone which the Liberator crossed in order to get Gan to medical attention.

**GRAVITY GENERATOR** – Total field generator developed by Thaarn. It was shielded by Herculanium, and in its complete form was designed to be able to move planets and stars.

**GRENLEE** – Federation Major in charge of security at Residence 1.

**GROFF** – Senior Technician to Thaarn. He was

originally on a Federation survey ship which was captured by Thaarn.

**GROSE** – Federation section leader on the planet Sardos. Previously a member of the 5th Legion, he, like his Legion, was noted for brutality.

**GROVANE** – Officer on board the Galaxy Class ship Ortega.

**GUN-SAR** – Chief of the Hommiks on the planet Xenon. The spelling of his name, as with all names on tribal planets, was flexible and appeared variously as Gunn Sar and Gun Sar.

**HANNA** – Addict of Shadow, encountered by the crew of Liberator in their search for the Terra Nostra.

**HARMON** – Federation trooper working under Klegg who helped take over the Liberator after the Intergalactic War.

**HASK** – Freedom Fighter working for Hunda on the planet Helotrix.

**HELIOFUSION ROD** – Used by Avon in his fight against Gun-Sar on the planet Xenon.

**HELOTRIX** – One of the oldest colonies, one of the first to gain independence from the Federation, and one of the earliest ones to be re-colonised. It was also known as Helotron.

**HELOTS** – Inhabitants of Helotrix, reputed to be very tenacious fighters, particularly able in hand-to-hand combat.

**HERCULANIUM** – Strongest known metal in the universe. It was an alloy which could not be cut, blasted or burnt through.

**HERON** – Frontier world on which climate control went wrong before the main attack by the Andromedans on Star One.

**HIGH INTENSITY RADIATION GRID** – Grid surrounding Control, the Federation central computer complex on Earth, which marked out the Forbidden Zone. The rays from the grid burnt people within seconds, and it had total self-repair within eight seconds.

**HIYTECHS** – Community on Chenga who hunted the savages for a bounty so that their bodies could be used in spare part surgery.

**HOB** – Comrade of Sula on Earth.

**HOFFAL'S RADIATION** – Radiation which occurred when neutrons were subjected to intense magnetic forces. Exposure to it caused rapid aging. It was responsible for the deaths of Egrorian and Pinder.

**HOME WORLD** – One of the names given by Kerril to the planet to which she and Vila were instantaneously transported from Keezarn.

**HOMMIKS** – One of the two tribes on Xenon. After a major war many hundreds of years before the arrival of Avon and the others the Hommiks, who were male-dominated and treated women as lesser creatures, banished almost all technology in an attempt to start their civilisation again in accordance with a decree of the Council of Survivors. However they continued to fight with the all-female Seska.

**HORIZON** – The only habitable planet within Zone 9 of the galaxy. Breathable atmosphere and Earth-type gravity.

**HOST** – Zil's name for its planet.

**HOWER** – First citizen on Obsidian.

**HULL SENSORS** – Part of the sensor system on the Liberator. It was the hull sensors that were damaged when the Liberator passed through liquid particles en route for Terminal, and it was this which led to the eventual destruction of the entire space ship.

**HUNDA** – Star Major, leader of the resistance on the planet Helotrix.

**HYPER SPACE SHIPS** – Mentioned by Ro, the puppet ruler of Horizon, as a new Federation development for travel to other galaxies. This would have involved speeds of up to TD50 for journeys outside the Local Group of galaxies (as those closely associated with our own are known.)

**HYPER SPACE SUB-BEAM** – Method of communication used by the Federation. The beam was converted into zeta 3 particles and thus became an unbreakable code.

**ICE CRYSTALS** – Used in heavy-duty lasers found on the unnamed planet in Series A Episode 9.

**IGIN** – Attached to the Fourth Column of the Freedom Fighters on the planet Helotrix.

**IMAGE AMPLIFIER** – Used by Hal Mellanby to restore his vision after the Federation had destroyed it during questioning.

**IMIPAK** – Induced Molecular Instability Projector and Key, developed by Coser. The weapon destabilised the individual; the key then completed the destabilisation and killed. The weapon only fired through a line of sight, but the key could be activated at any time thereafter and over exceptionally long distances. Despite its name having been taken from a set of initials, Imipak was sometimes spelled Imipac.

**IMPACT LIFE CAPSULE** – Many space craft carried these capsules so that in the event of serious damage to the space craft, the crew could eject. They were bullet shaped and meant to be able to withstand a drop from the very edge of the atmosphere onto a planetary surface. Minimal life support systems were inside.

**INBOARD SENSORS** – Range of sensors aboard the Liberator operated under the control of Zen.

**INERTIAL GUIDANCE GLYCOLENE BALLAST CHANNELS** – Part of the Anti-Grav Gyro System in Scorpio.

**INFRA-LUMINAL** – Power system used by Wanderer Class space ships.

**INNER WORLDS** – One of the two major sections under Federation administration.

129

**INSTANTANEOUS TRANSMISSION OF MATTER**
– System developed by the inhabitants of Keezarn at the height of their political, economic and technological growth three thousand years before the Liberator's arrival on the planet. The culture subsequently decayed into barbarism and the secret was only preserved in the City at the Edge of the World.

**INTERCEPTORS** – Federation space ships, which had reached Mark IV by the time Blake took over the Liberator.

**INTERGALACTIC DRIVE** – Theoretical drive presumably used by the Andromedans for their invasion.

**INTERGALACTIC WAR** – War between the Galaxy and Andromeda, set in motion after the aliens took over Star One and replaced the technicians there with their own kind. They were aided by Travis, who helped them dismantle the defences put up by the Federation after an Andromedan scout ship had been intercepted many years before. Although the war involved all planets in the galaxy, the bulk of the fighting was undertaken by the Federation, and as a result 80% of the Federation fleet was destroyed. Despite these losses the Federation finally won, mainly because it had more ships at its disposal than the Andromedans. A major contribution was made by Avon, who, commanding Liberator, held off a large portion of the invading fleet until Federation help was at hand.

**INTERPLANETARY MINING AGREEMENT** – Agreement which bound all mining companies to leave adequate power and fuel supplies on planets where mining had been abandoned.

**INTERROGATION DIVISION** – Division within the Federation armed forces.

**INVESTIGATOR** – Federation officer class which investigated both planets and individuals.

**IONIC BEAM** – Disabling beam used on space ships to cause minimum damage. An ionic beam could knock out Auron telepathic power.

**ISON** – Crystal which gave a space ship its vision; without it, the space ship flew blind.

**JARRIERE** – One of Servalan's underlings who went with her to Freedom City.

**JARVIK** – Construction worker who, during Servalan's attempts to capture the Liberator, expressed his disapproval of her tactical ability. He claimed he could take Liberator with one pursuit ship, which he subsequently did. He had formerly been a Captain in the Federation fleet, where he once had Tarrant in his crew. He later resigned from the Space Academy because of his dislike for the Federation's continual use of high technology. He was finally killed during a shoot-out on board Liberator after the Kairos affair.

**JENNA** – Native of Earth, full name Jenna Stannis. An expert space pilot, she was convicted of smuggling and sentenced to a penal colony, en route for which she met Blake. She clearly had a deep affection for Blake, although never adopting completely his political views. She went missing after leaving the Liberator in a life capsule during the Intergalatic War, and was reported by Zen as being on a hospital ship. On Gauda Prime, Blake stated that she died running a Federation blockade.

**JEVRON** – Planet on which, according to Servalan, Blake died one year before the meeting of Servalan and Avon on Terminal.

**COUNCILLOR JOBAN** – Elderly councillor, well-informed, willing and able to take a superior point of view against Servalan. He expressed dismay at the continued freedom of Blake and the Liberator crew.

**JUDGEMENT MACHINE** – Used in Federation courts to determine the innocence or guilt of those on trial.

131

**JUSTIN** – Genetic engineer and expert on radioactivity. He taught Dayna on Sarran before the war, but later became head of the Federation scientific warfare team. Killed by Servalan on Bucol 2.

**K47** – Wanderer Class I space ship that went missing in '61 Cygni (the Darkling Zone) 700 years prior to Blake's visit to Fosforon.

**KAARN** – Uninhabited planet to which the gene stocks of Auron were transported after the infection that had been spread by Servalan.

**KAINOSSES** – Independent Earth colony with a population of about 7 million.

**KAIROPAN** – Valuable material harvested on Kairos. Kairopan was used by large dangerous insect-like creatures to make silk.

**KAIROS** – Fourth planet of the star Zimonese in the constellation Lipterion, taking 15 years to travel round its sun. In its fertile zone, Kairopan was to be found.

**KARA** – Priestess on the planet Cygnus Alpha.

**KARLA** – Vandor agent who attempted to kill Deeta Tarrant on Teal Star.

**KASABI** – Main resistance leader on Earth. Kasabi was a senior political officer in Space Command who used her position teaching space cadets in order to preach treason. She was reported by Servalan and arrested. Kasabi then escaped and led the resistance, until she was contacted by Blake in his attempt to destroy Control on Earth.

**KASHALL THE WISE** – A figure in the legends of Cephlon, who in a dream saw that all life would end on the planet after the great wars. He devised a plan for ensuring the race's survival by preparing a space ship with dormant cells of the race. He was killed before he could put the plan into full operation, leaving his tribe to await the appearance of a new Lord.

**KATE** – Surviving member of the Seska on the planet Xenon.

**KAYN** – Neurosurgeon on XK72.

**KEEZARN** – Planet on which an ancient civilisation had developed and then declined.

**KEILLER** – Purser of the Space Princess who described Avon as an old friend, although Avon resisted this view of things. Keiller was employed by the Federation on the President's personal staff. He was used by Servalan in a plot to steal gold from Zerok and double-cross Avon.

**KELDA CITY** – Half its population was killed after Nova Queen crashed and its nuclear reactor went critical upon impact.

**DON KELLER** – Leader of first expedition to Virn. Servalan said that he had once been her lover.

**GINA KELLER** – Wife of Don Keller.

**KEMP** – Crew member of K47 Wanderer Class I space ship.

**KENDALL** – Doctor on board the Class III Galaxy Cruiser Ortega.

**CAPTAIN KENNEDY** – Captain on board the Space Princess.

**KERRIL** – Gunfighter working with Bayban who fell in love with Vila on Keezarn. Kerril was described by Bayban as 'the best gun hand I ever had.' She was transported to 'Vila-World' and eventually stayed there after Bayban's death.

**KIE-EYRE** – Name of Travis's mutoid pilot before she was transformed into a mutoid.

**KILLERS** – Miniature bombs which were placed in the gold being transported from Zerok. When the gold containers were opened, the Killers leapt out and attached themselves to living matter and then, some ten seconds later, exploded, thus killing anyone who happened to be trying to steal the gold.

**KLEGG** – Federation Section Leader who boarded the

Liberator after the Intergalactic War. He was killed by Dayna.

**KLINE** – Pseudonym adopted by Docholli after landing in Freedom City.

**KLUTE** – Diminutive alien working in the casinos of Freedom City playing chess. Whilst anyone beating or drawing with the Klute won 1 million credits, anyone losing was immediately electrocuted.

**KLYN** – Underling of Deva killed by Avon on Gauda Prime.

**KOMMISSAR** – Kommissars were installed on Federation colonies where local rulers were maintained as puppet rulers.

**KOSTOS** – Assistant of Servalan working on Terminal with Reeval. Kostos monitored Avon's walk across the planet to the shaft leading to the planet's interior.

**KRANTOR** – Head of an unnamed organisation on Freedom City. Krantor ran the main casino and quite probably Freedom City itself.

**KRELL** – Second man to transfer to Liberator from the London. He was sent mad but returned to the London.

**KRELL** – Senior Technician working on Centero. It was he who attacked Cally and led to the guards' giving the alarm during the raid on the base. (No apparent relation to the Krell on the London.)

**LAKON** – Cypher operative on Fosforon.

**LANGUAGE** – The Language used throughout the Federation and indeed the rest of the galaxy was Terran.

**LARGO** – Member of Terra Nostra organisation who wanted to employ Jenna on Callisto in order to transport drugs from there to Earth.

**LASER CANNON** – Weapon capable of blowing up an entire city, used by Bayban on Keezarn.

**LASER KNIVES** – Used to cut through any cable carrying a high energy charge. It was also possible to use an insulated saw.

**LASER PROBE** – Used as an instrument of torture by the Federation.

**LASER RIFLE** – Weapon used by the Federation.

**LAUNCH AND FLIGHT SIMULATOR (LFS)** – Used in the training of Federation pilots and by Belkov in his final game.

**LAUREN** — Sarran girl adopted by Hal Mellanby.

**LAZERON DESTROYER** – Powerful weapon attached to Travis's left hand so that he could kill instantly without having to keep a gun by his side. Travis used the weapon to injure Blake seriously on Star One.

**LECTOR** – Federation Unit Commander on Sardos.

**LEESAL RENOR** – One of the children supposedly molested by Blake, mentioned in his second trial.

**GOVERNOR LE GRAND** – Governor of the Outer Gow Region. Described by Avon as 'The only sane one amongst them'.

**LEHAN** – Ambassador from Aranon to Lindor who was charged with the responsibility of obtaining an alliance between the two planets so that both could resist the Federation more effectively.

**LEITZ** – Officer supplied by Commissioner Sleer to act as liaison between the puppet president of Helotrix and the Federation administration. He was a double agent, working for the Federation but pretending to be a resistance leader communicating information to Hunda. He was eventually killed by Servalan.

**LEVETT** – Officer on board the Galaxy Class ship Ortega.

**LEYLAN** – Commander of the ship London that transported Blake and the others to Cygnus Alpha.

**LIBERATOR** – Space ship found by the crew of London, drifting after a space battle. Blake, Jenna and Avon were sent on board to investigate the ship and subsequently commandeered it. It was much faster than anything in the Federation – its maximum speed was about Standard by 12, at which it could run for about two hours before all energy banks would be drained. Known to its manufacturers (The System) as Deep Space Vehicle 2, it contained upon discovery a wealth of clothing, currency and precious stones. It also contained advanced medical facilities, a massive store of food, a rapid re-generating system and a highly developed weaponry system.

LIFE – Most of the intelligent life forms encountered by the crew of the Liberator and Scorpio were humanoid, and it can be assumed that many had Earth ancestors. The Ultra claimed to have encountered millions of presumably intelligent species. Prime examples of non-humanoid life were the Core of Ultraworld and the aliens from Andromeda who invaded during the Intergalactic War. On Saurian Major there was a suggestion that the plants had an intelligence rating. The Decimas and the animal Og were the result of genetic engineering that produced intelligent life but with alien physical characteristics. The fact that the humanoids of Keezarn developed an exceptionally high culture long before Earth was civilised, and that a highly advanced alien civilisation was thought to exist in 61 Cygni within our galaxy, reveals that Earth was not the source of all sentient life. Of the more unusual life forms encountered was the unnamed planet in Series B Episode 6 which acted as a single organism. The oceans were made of saliva, and the creatures on the surface were treated as parasites and absorbed when they grew too numerous. Similarly unexpected was Virn, on which the sand was alive. It sucked out cellular energy from humans. Finally, just as many intelligent life forms evolved into humanoid patterns, so they subsequently evolved further whilst retaining some of the basic humanoid features. The Links on Terminal represent what mankind was to become millions of years from now. Likewise Moloch, a diminutive but just recognisably humanoid life form, represented what his humanoid ancestors were to become in millions of years time.

**LIFE-WORLD** – Artificial satellite maintained by the System computer.

**LIMITER** – Control system implanted in Gan's head by the Federation to stop him killing again after he had killed a Federation guard.

**LINDOR** – Neutral planet outside the Federation ruled by Sarkoff.

**THE LINDOR STRATEGY** – Plan organised by the Federation that commenced with the rigging of elections in order to remove President Sarkoff from power and was designed to eventually bring the planet into the Federation with Sarkoff as puppet leader. Blake found out about the Strategy after having stolen a Federation cypher machine.

**LINKS** – Ferocious creatures living on Terminal. The result of the Terminal Experiment, they represented what mankind was to become in the future.

**LIPTERIAN** – Space station used by Servalan.

**LIRAN** – One of the priests of Cygnus Alpha with an eye to promotion.

**LOCKS** – Opening locks was Vila's forte. The most complicated locks in use in the Federation were those coded with physio-psycho patterns. Anyone wishing to pass through something guarded with such a lock would be scanned by the door lock and, if the pattern fed into the central computer agreed with those permitted to enter, the door would open. The only way to break such a lock was to intercept the feedback from the computer. Less complex were the fingerprint locks – the computer recognised the correct fingerprints and, when it did so, opened the door. Such locks could be bypassed by presenting them with an impression of the correct fingerprints – covering a material that had been touched by the correct person with dust, placing some glass over

137

the dust, and then placing that glass on the fingerprint control. Voice recognition inputs built into locking mechanisms were described by Vila as being foolproof. Also encountered and opened by Vila were electrostatic locks using sonal keys, a Fantasol Lock where the key had built-in tangram codes, and Magno-locks, which he could open with difficulty.

**LOD** – Planetary leader brought into an alliance with Zukan, Boorva, Chalsa and Mida by Avon.

**LODESTAR** – Betafarl space ship which accompanied Zukan on his journey to the Summit meeting called by Avon.

**LONDON** – See Civil Administration Ship London.

**THE LONG COLD** – Six-year cycle of winter on the unnamed planet which was the scene of Series A Episode 9.

**LORN** – Tribal leader who found Vila on Chenga.

**THE LOST** – People in one of the legends of Auron. They were cast out by the Auronar as being unfit.

**THE LOST TIME** – Historic period on Goth, perhaps a time before its inhabitants moved into tribalism.

**L-TYPE CRUISER** – Small space ship of the type used by Servalan after losing the Presidency.

**LUBA** – Planet which re-entered the Federation by force after the Intergalactic War at the same time that Helotrix returned to the empire.

**LURENA** – Federation Officer on Star One. A friend of Durkim, she was the last unprogrammed human left during the Star One invasion.

**LURGEN** – Cyber-surgeon involved in the building of Star One. He was operated on by Docholli, but the operation was faked in order to leave Lurgen's brain intact. He was therefore the last person to know the location of Star One.

**LYE** – Guard positioned outside the courtroom during the trial of Travis.

**MAGDALEN ALPHA** – Star system to which it was projected that the rocket launched from the planet Cephlon by Avon would eventually land. The system had four planets with biospheres suitable for the development of humanoid life.

**MAGNETIC BARRIER** – Defence mechanism placed around Horizon.

**MAGNETRIX TERMINAL 406** – Refinery on the planet Helotrix. It acted as the Federation communications centre on that planet.

**MALL** – Friend of Lorn.

**MALODAAR** – Planet with methane and argon atmosphere and surface temperature around –90 to 100 degrees Centigrade. Used as a base by Egrorian.

**MANDRIAN** – Officer on board the Galaxy Class ship Ortega.

**MANGON** – Stew made from fungus, given to prisoners on Domo.

**MARAVIK** – Ruler of the Hommiks before Gun-Sar. He led the major battle against the Seska.

**MARK II STAR CRUISER** – Federation class of space ship used by Servalan after the Intergalactic War.

**MARYATT** – One of two Federation officers on an unnamed space ship on a secret mission which crashed into the planet Cephlon. Maryatt was a space surgeon in the Federation medical corps and was going to operate on Ensor as part of the Orac deal. He had previously saved Travis's life when Blake attempted to kill him.

**MAX** – Member of the diplomatic corps of the United Planets of Teal.

**MECRON 2** – Planet on which Belkov was based; centre of Feldon crystal mining.

**MECRONIANS** – Ancient civilisation on the planet Mecron. The high priests of the Mecronians used the Feldon crystals as a symbol of their power. The Mecronians had triangular knives which they used with deadly accuracy.

**MEDI-CAPSULE** – Central medical unit on Scorpio. It was fitted with a cryogenic chamber.

**MEEGAT** – Priestess on the planet Cephlon.

**HAL MELLANBY** – Fugitive from Earth and father of Dayna. He led a revolt some 15 years before the Freedom Party was formed, and when his followers were killed by Federation forces he fled with Dayna to Sarran where he was killed by Servalan.

**METEORITES** – Particles of stone or iron, usually little more than a metre across, moving freely in space in swarms. When encountered by a ship, they were called meteorite storms. They were measured on Liberator by scale and intensity – scale was a measurement of the area and intensity the number of meteorites within that area.

**MIDA** – Planetary leader brought into an alliance with Zukan, Boorva, Chalsa and Lod by Avon.

**MILUS** – Inhabitant of Obsidian killed by Mori. Brother of Nuti.

**MOLECULAR SHIFT DETECTOR** – Device rigged up by Escon to detect the large kinetic potential which was a side effect of all teleport communications. The device revealed exactly where and when Blake and the others would land.

**MOLOCH** – Master computer on the planet Sardos. Moloch was not only a computer, but also an organic being, the result of computer projection forward to show what his race would become 2 million years hence.

**MOLOK** – Criminal psychopath who worked for Travis.

**MONOPASIUM 239** – Ore mined on Horizon.

**MOON DISC** – Organic member of the Cactus family, main constituent of the drug Shadow. The cactus – also known as Alpha 7/5 – was prized for its partial telepathy. It could move short distances in order to avoid direct sunlight. The Moon Disc was rendered virtually extinct by commercial collectors. Normally three to six inches across, reddish-black in colour and flying-saucer shaped.

**ALTA MORAG** – Colleague of Doctor Havant working on Earth for the overthrow of Blake's credibility. Prosecuted Blake at his second trial.

**MORI** – Underling of Servalan when President to whom she once offered the Supreme Commander's position.

**MORPHANIEL** – Last known location of Jenna after the Intergalactic War.

**ELTON MULLER** – Taught by Ensor. He developed the master android which tried to link up with Orac in order to dominate the galaxy and enslave all humanoid life.

**VENA MULLER** – Wife of the cyberneticist. Killed by the android Muller.

**MUSIC** – Judging by the music that Cally was listening to in Series A Episode 12 whilst waiting by the teleport system, music seemed to have developed very little from its 20th-century form during the Federation. The music played on board the Space Princess also sounded like standard Musak from the 20th century. Religious music, where it was found (on Cygnus Alpha for example), was also little changed from its earlier equivalents.

**MUTOIDS** – Employed by Servalan and Travis as pilots. They only obeyed and did not question, and they lived on blood serum. They had been modified from complete human beings, but the memory of who they had been was erased after modification. They were thus reliable and, in Federation terms, expendable, but could be seen as a form of genetic engineering, which was of course forbidden.

**NAGU** – Aid to Governor Le Grand. Killed by Travis.

**NAPIER** – Assistant to Dr Plaxton on Caspar.

**NATRATOF OF GOURIMPEST** – Slave bidder who used a proxy on Domo.

**NAVIGATION COMPUTERS** – Part of the computer system aboard Liberator under the control of Zen.

**NEBROX** – Old man imprisoned with Avon on Domo.

**NEGATIVE UNIVERSE** – Theoretical universe presumed to exist on the other side of a black hole.

**NEURONIC WEB** – Light and sound weapon which could reduce a man to a gibbering idiot in seconds. It stopped all resistance and forced recipients to tell the truth.

**NEUTRON BLASTERS** – Main form of attack available to the Liberator. The neutron blaster had to be cleared before firing, thus taking up valuable seconds during battle manoeuvres. This function was carried out by Zen on instruction from a member of the crew. This problem had presumably not occurred with the Alta of the System – the Liberator's creator – since they were partially computerised themselves.

**NEUTRON FLARE SHIELD** – Had to be activated on Liberator before the neutron blasters could be cleared for firing.

**NEUTROTOPE** – The people of Destiny planned to put the neutrotope into orbit around their planet in order to deactivate certain rays from their sun so that the growing of crops would not be inhibited.

**NEW CALENDAR** – Started by the Federation at the time of the closing of the churches and banning of religion. By the time of Blake, it was the 2nd Century of the New Calendar.

**NINA** – Previous member of the Seska who had gone over to the Hommiks and was performing operations in their hospital through which Seska women were removed of their powers. She also became the wife of Gun-sar.

**NORL** – Leader of the people living near the City at the Edge of the World on the planet Keerzarn.

**NORM ONE** – Code name for a slave worker in the System who helped Blake escape when trapped by

System guards. Norm One killed Alta 2, but was himself soon killed by System guards.

NOVA – Convict who worked with Blake, Jenna, Avon, Vila and Gan to take over the ship London whilst it was transporting them all to Cygnus Alpha. Nova however was killed during the operation – had he lived he would certainly have been the eighth member of the Liberator crew.

NOVA QUEEN – Passenger space ship which crashed with 4000 passengers on board as a result of a malfunction in the computers on Star One.

NOVARA – Member of the renegade Auronar who built the Web.

NUCLEAR COMPRESSION CHARGE – Highly effective explosive device which made a miniature black hole, thus sucking in all matter around it.

NUCLEAR PLASMIC ABSORPTION – Process used on Ultraworld along with Germainian circuitry which enabled the planet to exist as a living being and expand. The process worked through cellular regeneration.

NUCLEIC BURSTER – Radiation flare with a very high radiation level.

NUTI – Inhabitant of Obsidian killed by Mori. Brother of Milus.

OBSIDIAN – Planet in a strategic position in the 6th Sector with breathable atmosphere but a large active volcano near the main settlement. The planet was contaminated by radioactive fallout from a nuclear device buried in its core that was intended as a threat against invading forces. The inhabitants used behavioural psychology to remove all aggressive instincts from themselves. Thus, despite its being surveyed by the Federation and subsequently caught in the middle of the Intergalactic War, it survived and retained its independence. However when the Federation attacked it under Servalan's orders, Hower detonated the nuclear device and destroyed the planet.

**OG** – Genetically engineered animal created by Justin, able to work within areas of high radioactivity. He was killed by Servalan on Bucol 2.

**ONUS 2** – Planet regularly visited by Dorian in order to provide nutrients for the Seska's food-processing plant.

**OPEN PLANET** – Planet on which the penal code was suspended in order to speed up the exploitation of resources.

**ORAC** – Computer invented by Ensor which had the ability to tap all other computers through the use of a standard component, also invented by Ensor, found in every computer in the galaxy – the Tarriel Cell. Orac used special communication waves that passed into a fifth dimension, the same dimension which allows thought transference. However, Orac had no consciousness in that dimension and was thus not telepathic. It enjoyed playing Galactic Monopoly, disliked work it considered unnecessary, loved gathering information and had delusions of grandeur. Orac could actually take over other computers and force them to obey its commands. Indeed according to its inventor, Orac was more than a computer, it was a brain. Nevertheless it had definite limitations to its capacity to take in information. Orac was severely damaged to the extent of ceasing operation in the explosions caused by Zukan on Xenon base, but was sufficiently repaired by Avon to be able to track down Blake to Gauda Prime. Orac was not seen during the final shoot-out on the planet, presumably having been left outside the base in a safe place.

**ORBITER** – Space ship of Belkov, the first ship ever to be powered by Feldon crystals.

**ORTEGA** – Galaxy Class space ship which should have been en route for Destiny but was found by

Liberator moving round in circles.

**THE OUTER DARKNESS** – Area of space near the planet Calcos, so named by the early pioneers of space flight. An area in which there were no known stars.

**THE OUTER PLANETS** – Location referred to as the place where Blake's parents settled. These planets were at the furthest limit of space colonised by Earthmen, but were not part of the Federation. They tended to be taken over by the Federation if they were found to be of strategic, mineral or other value.

**OUTER WORLDS** – One of the two major administrative areas of the Federation.

**OUTSIDERS** – People on Earth who lived illegally outside the Great Domes.

**PACIFICATION AND CONTROL PROGRAMME** – Programme in the control of Servalan (under the name of Commissioner Sleer) which was used to subjugate dissident populations during the re-colonisation programme after the Intergalactic War. It was based on the use of the drug Pylene 50, which blocked the production of adrenalin and thus to some degree changed the personality. Populations affected by the drug continued to work normally but ceased to resist the Federation. The programme was very similar to that used on Earth to keep the populace there under control.

**PAIR BOND** – Goth phrase for marriage.

**PALMERO** – Frontier world and the Federation's main producer of tropical fruit.

**PAR** – Federation Trooper who served under Travis for 5 years. He visited Travis at his Court Martial.

**PARAFLAME 5** – Lethal gas, normally used as a coolant. It was released on Xenon base after the explosions created by Zukan.

**PARATYPE 926** – Alien disease which attacked cells altered by Terran Ague and caused rapid death. As

Terran Ague was caused only by flying in deep space, the disease only killed humans who had left Earth and was thus an attempt to keep mankind there.

**PARTICLE DRIVER CONTROL** – Part of the Photonic Drive.

**PARTON** – Federation Officer on Star One who was taken over by the aliens before the Intergalactic War.

**PASCO** – Officer on board the Galaxy Class ship Ortega.

**PATAR** – Flight Controller on Auron.

**PAURA** – Native of the planet Horizon. Blake met Paura on a Federation convict ship en route for the planet Cygnus Alpha.

**PAYTER FEN** – One of the children who had supposedly been molested by Blake, which alleged offence resulted in his second trial.

**PELLA** – Leader of the Seska.

**PETROSCOPE** – Device used by Avon in searching for crystals.

**PHAROS** – Base of the Robot Development Cartel from which Muller was to be rescued.

**PHOBON PLAGUE** – Scientifically incorrect name of a virus type which was used by Servalan and Travis in an attempt to kill the entire crew of the Liberator. The mutated version they used had a particularly short life cycle and was self-eliminating.

**PHOTONIC DRIVE** – Developed by Dr Plaxton, it used light instead of plasma to develop thrust. The Mark II went up to TD 15 in real time.

**PHOTOPRINT RECORD** – Federation record held on all citizens.

**PILOT 40** – Auron pilot captured by Servalan and used to introduce a disease onto Auron.

**PINDER** – Brilliant mathematician who worked for Egrorian. He was affected by exposure to Hoffal's Radiation and thus appeared to be in his late seventies when actually only twenty-eight. He used the radiation to kill Egrorian and himself.

**PIRI** – Hired female assassin known as Cancer who used crabs to kill her victims.

**PLACE OF REBIRTH** – Location of religious importance on Cygnus Alpha.

**PLANET HOPPER** – Space ship travelling between planets within a solar system, as opposed to other ships which travelled between the stars.

**PLANTATION 5** – Area of Gauda Prime on which Scorpio crashed.

**PLASMA BOLTS** – Main weapon used by Federation Pursuit Ships. Huge balls of glowing, superheated fusion reaction power. Unprotected objects were instantly vapourised. The maximum number of plasma bolts ever fired at one time were the four fired by Travis in Series A Episode 8.

**PLASMA RADIATION** – Inevitable side effect of using main thrust on Scorpio.

**DR PLAXTON** – Head of Federation Space Drive Research Centre, inventor of Photonic Drive. She died on board Scorpio fitting the new drive.

**PLUTONIC POWER CELLS** – Power cells used by the exiled Auronar, diminished when Blake met them at the time that Liberator was caught in the Web. The cells were used to keep the life-support systems going and needed recharging from time to time.

**POOLA** – Inhabitant of Sardos.

**PRACTOR** – President-elect of the planet Helotrix at the time of Scorpio's visit to the planet. He was a Helot who had been on the Federation Civil List for many years.

**PRECISION GUIDANCE SUBSYSTEM** – Part of the Scorpio control system operated by Slave.

**PRESIDENT** – Ruler of the Federation. Full title: President of the Terran Federation, Ruler of the High Council, Lord of the Inner and Outer Worlds, High Admiral of the Galactic Fleets, Lord General of the

Six Armies and Defender of Earth. For a period around the time of the Intergalactic War, Servalan was President.

**PRIMITIVES** – Tribesmen on Chenga who were Hunted by the Hi Techs so that their bodies could be used in the organ banks. Whilst adopting a simple lifestyle by choice, they were not primitive in their understanding of technology.

**PROBABILITY SQUARE** – Method of analysing problems, used by Avon. It involved representing each element of a problem by a cube, and moving the cubes in relation to each other so that new and previously unthought-of interactions could be perceived.

**PROGRAMMED GUARDIANS** – Humanoids found on the time capsule in Series A Episode 4. They were programmed to destroy anyone they met after coming out of their cryogenic chambers who might threaten the gene banks they carried. The banks could be incubated and produce a complete adult in 1.6 minutes.

**PROHIBITED SPACE ZONES** – Zones of space which contained such dangers that they were impossible to travel through in normal space ships.

**PROVINE** – Space Major on the planet Albian, in charge of the Federation Space Assault Force. Provine served with Central Control before taking on this assignment. He was believed by Blake to know the location of the computer complex Control, and in fact it was Provine who first told Blake that Control was on Star One.

**PROVUS 4** – Planet of origin of Relf, whom Tarrant met in Ultraworld.

**PSYCHOMANIPULATION** – Federation method of brain control.

**PSYCHOSTRATEGY** – Art of predicting what individuals would do on the basis of their psyches. Psychostrategists aimed to take everyone and everything into account and thus were not only able to make calculated guesses as to the future but also, through the manipulation of environments, had the power to force people into taking certain specific actions. This method only went wrong if vital information was not available to the Psychostrategist, as when Carnell predicted that Coser would go mad after stealing Imipak. This didn't happen because Coser had a companion with him, and Carnell's psychostrategy was based on Coser being alone. Known colloquially as 'puppeteers' and held in awe by lower ranks because of their supposed power to both predict and influence the actions of others.

**PUPPETEERS** – Colloquial term for Psychostrategists.

**PURSUIT SHIPS** – The most rapid space ships available to the Federation, often used in attempts to track the Liberator. Servalan used a modified Type 1 Pursuit Ship. By the time of Series C, the Federation had got up to Mark 10 Pursuit Ships, which had modified fins for greater time distort facility and were based on the Hunter-Killer Class.

**PYLENE 50** – Drug that was at the heart of the Pacification Programme used on Helotrix and elsewhere after the Intergalactic War. It had the disadvantage that it was only stable for a few days and thus had to be made on the planet on which it was to be used. In normal quantities it was a muscle relaxant, and only when the normal dose was multiplied a hundredfold did its new properties come to light. By the end of Series D, the Federation were pumping Pylene 50 into reservoirs and the atmospheres of all planets on which they were taking control.

**PYROANS** – Inhabitants of Obsidian.

**PYRRUS** – Star described by Keiller as being a ferocious power, the twelfth wonder of the galaxy.

**Q-BASE** – Federation base on Fosforon.

**QUADRANT** – The galaxy was divided into eight

quadrants for easy reference. These were similar to, but different from, the Zones and Sectors.

**QUUTE** – Colonel with the Federation forces on Helotrix.

**RACE MEMORY** – Memory held subconsciously by all members of a race. Race memory could be genetically engineered so that an entire race would perform a certain act at a certain time.

**RAFFORD** – Pilot on the Class 3 Galaxy Cruiser Ortega who was killed prior to the arrival of the Liberator.

**RAI** – Federation Officer under the command of Servalan. Rai and Servalan were described by Servalan as being 'old friends'.

**RAIKER** – Sub-Commander on board the space ship London which transported Blake to Cygnus Alpha. It was Raiker who made the initial suggestion that Blake, Jenna and Avon should transfer to the Liberator after the death of Teague and Krell.

**RAKOFF** – First Champion of the Vandor Confederacy prior to Vinni.

**RALLI** – Female resistance leader on Albian.

**RASHEL** – Slave who accompanied Coser when he stole Imipak. After the defeat of Servalan, she remained on the uninhabited planet with the Clone-Blake.

**RATS** – Rats existed on all colonised planets, the only life form other than man to be so widespread.

**RAVELLA** – Friend of Blake who, with Richie, took him outside the Dome on Earth, thus setting off the series of events which led to his second trial.

**REAL TIME** – Time distort travel involved a jump out of the dimension in which the speed of time is fixed dependent on the speed of travel (as experienced on Earth for example, and as explained by Einstein) into another dimension in which the two were not related. Real time travel was the opposite of this – the traveller stayed within the normal dimension, and thus time moved backwards when the traveller moved faster than light. The drive developed by Dr Plaxton was sensational because it actually achieved the speeds of the Liberator in real time – that is, without going into time distort. This apparently broke all the laws of physics as expounded by Einstein.

**REEVAL** – Assistant of Servalan working with Kostos on Terminal. Reeval monitored Avon's walk across the planet to the shaft that led to its interior.

**REEVE** – Federation Investigator who led the second expedition to Virn.

**RELAXANT** – Drug designed for medicinal purposes only, but much favoured by Vila after stress (when he could get hold of it).

**RELF** – Inhabitant of Provus 4 who, after capture by the Ultra, was placed in a tube as a specimen and used as a menial when needed.

**RELIGION** – The Federation had all churches destroyed at the start of the New Calendar, between one and two hundred years before Blake. Although religion was apparently outlawed on Earth and presumably throughout the Federation, it existed in primitive forms in many other places, as for example on Mecron, where the Feldon crystals formed a major part of the religious beliefs of the Mecronians. It is interesting to note the strong similarity between the religious chants used by the Mecronians and those used on Cygnus Alpha.

**REMOTE LOCK ACTIVATOR** – Mechanism used for opening hatches of space ships where one does not have the necessary electronic device.

**RENOR** – Assistant to Kayn the neurosurgeon.

**REPLICATION PLANT** – Centre of genetic replication on Auron, as invented by Franton.

**RESIDENCE 1** – Servalan's headquarters on Earth after she took over the Presidency.

**RICHIE** – Friend of Blake who took him outside the

Dome on Earth and thus started the train of events leading to Blake's second trial. Richie revealed to Blake details about his past which enabled Blake to break through the mind blocks set by the Federation before his first trial.

**RIDDLES** – Orac expressed an interest in the idiosyncratic syntax of riddles. His interest in them, combined with Vila's ability to tell them, saved the crew of the Liberator from the Ultra.

**RO** – Puppet ruler of the planet Horizon.

**ROBOT DEVELOPMENT CARTEL** – Civil organisation within the Federation.

**ROD** – Brother of Gola, tribal chief of Goth.

**RONTANE** – Secretary and personal representative of the President before the Intergalactic War.

**RULE OF LIFE** – Rule by which the Clonemasters governed their science. It forbade the making of clones for aggressive purposes and stated that 'all life is linked'.

**SAMOR** – Senior Federation General who was in charge of the trial at which Travis was sentenced to death. Also known as Star Killer.

**SARA** – Officer on board the Galaxy Class ship Ortega. She stole the neutroscope in order to sell it to the highest bidder, and killed three crew members of the ship that carried it in the process of so doing.

**SARDOS** – Large fixed meteoroid supporting a population of 300. The inhabitants undertook exhaustive projections into their own future and, as a result, decided to avoid any genetic contact with outsiders so as to stop the evolutionary process.

**SARKOFF** – President of Lindor kept in exile on an uninhabited planet whilst the Federation tried to annex Lindor.

**SARRAN** – Planet on which Dayna and Hal Mellanby lived. It was dominated by primitive tribesmen led by Chel.

**SAURIAN MAJOR** – Self-governing planet in Star Sector 46.21, annexed by the Federation. A subsequent rebellion was quashed, with half the population killed and the rest transported. A small number remained as guerilla bands. All Federation signals were sent via Saurian Major to boost their power. It had a day that lasted approximately thirty-six hours, plants that were carnivorous and some that had an intelligence rating. It was there Blake met Cally, who after the raid joined the crew of Liberator.

**SAYMON** – Corporate indentity kept in a solution on the unnamed planet to which Blake and Avon teleported in Series A Episode 5. It consisted of exiles from Auron, and by the time Blake met it Saymon was a summary of six separate identities within one mind.

**SCAVENGERS** – People on Cephlon were divided into two tiny groups: the Scavengers, who were savages, and those still living inside the dome, who were led by Meegat.

**SCHOLERIANS** – Space ship builders who were renowned for their ability at stealing designs and copyright patterns from each other and from other space ship builders and designers.

**SCORPIO** – Wanderer Class planet-hopper Mark II which underwent enormous modification under the direction of Dorian. It was taken over by Avon et al and used until it crashed on Gauda Prime. Unlike Liberator, pressurised doors sealed off all areas of Scorpio from the flight deck when in space. The ship was under the general control of the computer Slave.

**SECTOR** – The known galaxy was divided into 12 Sectors for ease of reference. Each Sector was then subdivided into ten Sub-sectors, which were in turn divided into 99 Regions. Thus Saurian Major was in Sector 46.21 – Sector 4, Sub-sector 6, Region 21. This was a more precise reference system than the

Zones and Quadrants, which were not sub-divided.

**SECTOR 4** – Contained the planet Helotrix.

**SECTOR 6** – Contained the artificial planet Terminal.

**SECTOR 11** – Area of space beyond the edge of the galaxy which included Star One but little else.

**SECTOR 12** – One of the two spiral arms on the edge of the galaxy. It was uncharted, and Federation ships sent to survey the area rarely returned. The System (builders of Liberator) was located in this Sector.

**SEEDING** – The placing of mines in random orbit around a planet.

**SEEKERS** – Explosive devices on Liberator which, when fired, would seek out nearby enemy ships and, although unlikely to destroy them, would certainly knock them off course.

**SELMA** – Native of the planet Horizon who was going to marry Ro. When she refused to undertake Federation training, she was sent to the mines as a slave.

**SELSON** – Member of the Federation Space Assault Force on Albian.

**SENSORMET** – System that used microsensors implanted in the brains of the Champions of Teal and Vandor in combination with a mesh in the skull. Signals from the champions' brains were transmitted to the combat computers and then on to anyone wearing a Sensormet via the wearer's optic nerve.

**SENSORY ECSTASY HOURS** – Form of relaxation much valued by Vila, found at Federation Rest Centres.

**SERKASTA** – Planet on which Travis was alleged to have murdered 1417 unarmed civilians.

**SERVALAN** – Native of Earth. Having started out as a cadet, she became Supreme Commander of Space Command. Prior to the Intergalactic War she ousted the President and installed herself as total ruler. She was deposed during her enforced isolation on Terminal and adopted the name Sleer, having been rumoured killed during a rear-guard action on Gedden. Using drug control, she initiated a massive conquest of planets which Avon tried to stop.

**SESKA** – One of the two tribes on Xenon. The Seska consisted entirely of women who were experts in tele-ergonomics and had helped Dorian with his various research projects on Xenon. The Seska had supposedly been working on the teleport for generations before the arrival of the survivors of the Liberator.

**SHAD** – Federation space pilot involved in shuttling harvested Kairopan away from the planet.

**SHADOW** – Drug that was the major source of finance for the Terra Nostra. It was derived from an organic compound of the Cactus family, Species Alpha 7/5. Described by the President of the Federation as 'the greatest single threat to the welfare of mankind', the Shadow operation (and hence the Terra Nostra) was in fact run by the President of the Federation.

**SHERM** – Lieutenant to Bayban, the Federation's most wanted criminal.

**SHEVRON** – Name used by Avon when re-boarding the Liberator after the Intergalactic War.

**SHIVAN** – Original member of the Freedom Party presumed dead, whose identity Travis took over in an attempt to capture Blake.

**SHRINKER** – Federation prison guard on Earth specialising in torture. He told Avon of the existence of Bartolomew and was then left to die in an underground cavern on Earth.

**SINGLE ISOMORPHIC RESPONSE** – The guns on the Liberator originally carried this device, presumably to enable each member to have a gun which no-one else would be able to take. Anyone trying to take the wrong gun found it very hot to the touch.

**SINOFAR** – Guardian of the Power. Worked with Giroc, together the sole survivors of a race which destroyed itself after thousands of years of warfare. The aim of Sinofar was to 'dissipate the Power by restoring the Balance'.

**SIXTY-ONE CYGNI** – One of the first stars whose distance from Earth was measured accurately in the 19th century. By Blake's time it was the only area of space near Earth that remained unsurveyed. The K47 Wanderer Class space ship went missing in its area. It was the home of an advanced alien life form.

**DOCTOR SLATEN** – Doctor on board the Space Princess.

**SLAUGHTERHOUSE** – Unofficial name for the reception area on Chenga where patients were kept ready for use in the organ bank.

**SLAVE** – Master computer on the space ship Scorpio, built and programmed by Dorian. It had a cringing personality, addressing Avon as 'Master' and others as 'Sir' or 'Madam'. It apologised continually and was occasionally reduced to panic, concluding its journey to Gauda Prime with the statement, 'The ground is very close, Sir'.

**SLAVERY** – Existed on Federation planets and in the System. Also used by Lord Thaarn on his artificial planet Crandor, and on Ultraworld. A form of slavery was organised by the pirates on Domo, who captured passing space ship passengers and sold them to the highest bidder.

**SLEER** – Pseudonym adopted by Servalan after she lost the Presidency and started work as a Commissioner in Federation Security.

**SOLIUM RADIATION DEVICE** – Deadly device which caused destruction of all living tissue over a very wide area. It was used by the Federation as its final threat against the inhabitants of Albian. Solium produced a small explosion and the resultant radiation decayed within twenty-four hours. It left all buildings intact whilst destroying all living matter, and was thus very similar in style to the neutron bomb of the 20th century.

**SOMA** – Intoxicating drink that played an important part in the ancient Vedic religion of India, taken from the juice of the plant Asclepias acida. It formed a constituent part of the liquid 'adrenalin and soma' much favoured by Vila on board Liberator.

**SONA VAPOUR** – Form of tranquilising gas, used on board the Galaxy Class cruiser Ortega.

**SONHEIM** – Officer on board the Galaxy Class ship Ortega.

**SOOLIN** – Two stories exist concerning Soolin's origins. According to one, she was a native of Earth who moved to Darlon IV with her family, who were murdered 6 years later. Aged 17, she killed her parents' murderers and left the planet to wander the galaxy, linking up with Dorian before becoming a member of Scorpio's crew. In the other version the events just described were said to have taken place on Gauda Prime, and there she was apparently killed along with Tarrant, Vila and Dayna.

**SOPRON** – Silicon-based substance registering high electronic activity, with a function similar to that of a capacity-charged brain. A rock of Sopron was gathered by Vila and Avon, who described it as the most sophisticated life form 'that it has ever been my good fortune to come across'. Sopron lived permanently on the dark side of its planet and as a defence mechanism reflected an image of anything that happened to be scanning it, the image always being slightly larger or slightly more powerful than its original. Avon built an analogue replica of Sopron and used it upon Liberator when the ship was controlled by Servalan, so that Zen thought it was looking at a ship more powerful than the Liberator itself.

**SOUNI** – Frontier world on which climate control broke down before the main attack on Star One.

**SPACE CHOPPER** – Small space ship outlawed by the Federation after becoming a teenagers' craze, and subsequently used by the Space Rats.

**SPACE CITY** – Entertainment satellite also known as the Satellite of Sin. Run by the Terra Nostra.

**SPACE COMMAND** – Military wing of the Federation of which Servalan was Supreme Commander. It was based on a space station near Earth.

**SPACE COMMANDER** – Senior rank in the Federation, commanding Pursuit Ships. Commanders reported directly to the Federation Supreme Commander.

**SPACE MASTER** – Small type of space craft used by the Federation. It was a Space Master that crashed into Cephlon, alerting the crew of Liberator and eventually leading to the gaining of Orac.

**SPACE PRINCESS** – Space craft on which Keiller was the purser. A pleasure ship used for transporting gold.

**SPACE RATS** – Encountered in Series D Episode 3 and described thus by Vila: 'All they live for is space and violence, booze and speed. And the fellows are just as bad.' They stole from transport museums after the banning of leisure transport and adopted the philosophy, 'If it moves, zap it.'

**SPACIAL** – Unit for the measurement of distance used on Liberator. Asteroid PK118 had a diameter of 0.102 spacials. Assuming this was equal to about 100 miles (asteroids are rarely bigger than 400 miles in diameter, and 100 is common), a spacial would be about 1000 miles. Liberator's standard orbit around a planet was 1000 spacials, which at about 1 million miles would put it beyond the orbit of the majority of natural moons and offer the possibility of rapid departure from a system in the event of trouble.

**SPEED** – Federation ships measured speed in Time Distort Units, the Liberator in multiples of its Standard Speed, with Standard by 1 possibly being equal to about TD4. Given certain known factors, such as the distance across the galaxy (which was a feasible journey in months rather than years) and the distance from our galaxy to Andromeda (which was not possible, even for the Liberator), the following assumptions can be made based on the universal constant, the speed of light (c): TD1 = 1000c, TD2 = 2000c, TD3 = 3000c, etc. Liberator could, for very short spells, achieve the equivalent of TD16. However at Standard by 7 (TD11), it would take just under one year to reach the centre of the galaxy from Earth, but over 200 years to reach Andromeda. The Star Drive II used on Scorpio could reach eveh higher speeds in the laboratory, going to TD15 in real time, which meant staying in the same time dimension as experienced on a planet rather than moving into a time-distorted dimension. It was also suggested that the Federation was developing an Intergalactic Drive which would clearly have involved much higher Time Distort speeds.

**SPEED CHESS** – Gambling game played against the Klute on Freedom City in which each contestant had five seconds to make a move.

**STABILISED ATOMIC IMPLOSION** – Method of reducing matter in size, used by Orac.

**STAR BURST** – Ship confined to the galactic Eighth Fleet. All three of the Star Burst Pursuit ships were requisitioned by Travis.

**STAR DRIVE MACHINE** – Photonic Drive.

**STARDUST BLIZZARD FIELD** – Harmless electrical phenomenon in space.

**STAR KILLER** – Nickname for Samor.

**STAR ONE** – Automatic computer control centre of the Federation in the Eleventh Sector which replaced Control on Earth. It represented the totality of Federation Control before the Intergalactic War. Situated between two galaxies, the Star One complex was built on a single planet circling a white dwarf star. Surface temperature was low and the main installation was underground. Star One was destroyed in an alien counter-atack during the Intergalactic War.

**STAR QUEEN** – Civilian cruiser encountered by the Liberator whilst in orbit around the unnamed planet on which President Sarkoff was being held.

**STARS** – Stars were classified into various types, although these classifications were rarely referred to by the crew of Liberator or by the Federation. The star around which the planet in Series A Episode 8 revolved was classified by Jenna as G2. For astronomical information, see the Introduction to the Index.

**STATIONARY ORBIT** – Orbit maintained in such a way that a space ship was constantly above one particular point on a planet.

**STOCK EQUALISATION ACT** – Federation law which ensured that when a planet was colonised, each race from Earth had to be fully represented in order to give a complete racial mix.

**STOT** – Federation Officer on Star One who was taken over by aliens before the Intergalactic War.

**STRATEGY 3** – Instruction given by Blake to Zen for the avoidance of Federation Pursuit Ships.

**SUB-BEAM** – Method of communication which could be used by the Liberator.

**SUBMUTONIC OVERLAP SHIFT** – Part of the process used for transmuting gold into black gold.

**SUBTERRANS** – Humanoid creatures living in caves on the unnamed planet that was the scene of Series A Episode 9. They were used as a slave labour force for mining ice crystals.

**SULA** – Also known as Anna Grant and Bartolomew. Married to High Councillor Chesku, whom she killed, and former girlfriend of Avon, whom she betrayed. He eventually killed her.

**THE SYSTEM** – Computer complex which controlled Life-World and three planets. These three planets were originally at war, but one of them evolved a massive computer which could take over the weaponry systems of the others and hence became dominant. That computer became the System, which governed from then on. It also developed at least two deep-space ships, one of which was Liberator.

**T16 – TYPE SPACE TRANSPORTER** – Widely used by the Federation. It carried no armament and no scanning devices.

**TACHYON FUNNEL** – Weapon invented by Egrorian which could destroy matter instantly at any range. It was based on a theoretical faster-than-light particle, the Tachyon. First postulated by Einstein, among other things it always moves backwards in time and loses energy as it accelerates.

**TAK** – Junior officer working under Tynus on Fosforon.

**TANDO** – Bounty hunter on Gauda Prime, killed by Blake

**TARA** – Sister of Gola, tribal ruler on Goth. She had a certain amount of prophetic and hypnotic powers and used them effectively on Jenna.

**DEL TARRANT** – Native of Earth and graduate of the Federation Space Academy. Posted as missing along with a Federation Pursuit ship, which he subsequently used to run contraband in the Outer Planets. He was thus on the Federation's wanted list at the time he boarded Liberator. He had one brother – Deeta. Tarrant was impetuous, brave, a bully and capable of quite mindless activity, as when he stopped Avon from putting on a space suit to survive the entry into a presumed black hole on the principle that the crew should all die together.

**DEV TARRANT** – Colleague of Doctor Havant. Tarrant worked in security, infiltrated the Freedom

Party and reported back to the administration.

**TARRIEL CELL** – Development by Ensor at the age of 18 which led to a completely new generation of computers, all of which contained one such cell. It was this unification of development that allowed Orac to tap any computer in the galaxy.

**TARSIUS** – Federation planet that was subjugated by use of the Pacification Programme under the guidance of Servalan.

**TARVIN** – Amagon pirate who captured the Liberator. He had known Jenna previously on Zolaf 4.

**TEAGUE** – First man from the space ship London to cross through the transfer tube from London to the Liberator. He was killed almost immediately.

**TEAL** – See the United Planets of Teal.

**TEAL STAR** – Liner on which Deeta Tarrant was travelling when war was declared between Teal and Vandor.

**TEAL-VANDOR CONVENTION** – Convention which eliminated war by decreeing that battles between the two peoples be fought out by champions within areas chosen by computer. The losing side had to give up two-thirds of its fleet and three planets.

**TECHNICIAN 241** – Worked in Section 3 of the Robot Development Cartel, and discovered Muller's headless body.

**TELE-ERGOTRON** – Controlled throughput of pure energy developed by the Seska.

**TELEKINESIS** – Method of moving objects with the power of the brain. According to Tarrant, telekinesis was unworkable because the brain did not generate enough energy. However Orac showed that with the use of energy stored elsewhere in the body and the brain directing that energy, telekinesis could in fact be accomplished. The Seska on Xenon had developed the ability of telekinesis through the use of an ingrafted co-radiating crystal which focused the beam.

**TELEMETRIC BAND SWEEP** – Command given by Tarrant, with no explanation provided.

**TELEPORT** – System of dismantling organic molecules, transporting them across space and then reassembling them. Non-organic molecules that were closely associated with organic molecules (eg, items of clothing) were also automatically teleported. The teleport system on Liberator worked on medium frequencies, but it was possible to adjust the teleport to work on omicron pulse length when there was interference on the medium band. Bracelets had to be worn to make the system work. On Liberator these were very fragile indeed and had clearly been designed for use by the Alta of the System. They included sensors which warned of the presence of poison gas or radiation. Scorpio's bracelets were much sturdier and became the personal property of each crew member. They were made of titanium and had chips set in a rack with a keyboard so that the landing site could be programmed into the bracelet.

**TERLOC** – Associate of Avalon who betrayed her to the Federation.

**TERMINAL** – Artificial planet built by a consortium of scientists 411 years before the Liberator was destroyed within its vicinity. According to official records, Terminal was supposed to have broken up many years prior to that. Terminal was sprayed with organic materials in the hope that it would naturalise and eventually create and sustain life. Originally positioned in solar orbit near Mars, it was somehow moved to a totally new location. Despite apparently being egg-shaped, the planet retained a breathable atmosphere and Earth-type gravity level. The question of how much of Terminal was colonised remains unresolved. Servalan merely occupied what appeared to be a few rooms underground, although there were further signs of habitation and building elsewhere on the planet.

These may, of course, have been built by the Links before they evolved into the aggressive creatures that were met by the crew of Liberator.

**TERRAN AGUE** – Metabolic reaction to space travel suffered by all humans. It altered the body's nucleic structure.

**TERRA NOSTRA** – Organisation similar to the 20th-century Mafia (or 'Cosa Nostra') which had infiltrated the entertainment, smuggling and drug rackets on almost all civilised worlds in the galaxy, running Space City among other things. The Terra Nostra worked in secret on the worlds controlled by the Federation, organising crime on a galaxy-wide basis.

**THAARN** – Creature from children's tales on Auron, one of the seven gods who discovered the land and created the people. The gods promised telepathy, but Thaarn, being jealous of this, killed another god and was sent beyond space and time, thus becoming a symbol of darkness and evil on Auron. In fact he went to Crandor and built a gravity generator which attracted the Liberator.

**THANIA** – Federation Major who defended Travis at his trial.

**THREE-DAY SWEAT** – Popular name for Terran Ague.

**THRILLS** – Gambler on Freedom City who played Speed Chess against the Klute and lost.

**TIME DISTORT** – Time Distort travel involved jumping out of the familiar dimension in which the speed of time is fixed with relation to the speed of travel into another dimension in which the two were unrelated. Consult the discussion of Real Time and Speed.

**TIME SHIFT** – Two modes of time shift were possible on the Liberator, Venir and Modula. The functional difference was never explained.

**TIME UNIT** – Approximately equivalent to a 24-hour day on Earth.

**TINCTURE OF PYRELLIC** – Poison used on Forbus by Commissioner Sleer. It was made from an extract of Papperalian fungi and had the effect of crippling and eventually killing. There was an antidote which stopped the poison spreading, but no complete cure.

**TOBER** – Crew member of K47 Wanderer Class I space ship discovered near Fosforon.

**TOISE** – Underling of Krantor.

**TP CRYSTAL** – Part of the A-line Converter in the Federation code system. It ran the spectrum from Band L to Y up to 30,000 MHz. Blake needed it to break the code system.

**TRANSFERENCE** – Method employed by the Ultra to remove personality profiles from an individual and store them in the memory of Ultraworld. Transference was the necessary process which preceded absorption.

**TRANSFER TUBE** – Flexible tube used by small Federation space ships for transfer from one ship to another through deep space.

**TRANSMUTATION OF METAL** – Achieved on Zerok, where the atomic matter of gold was changed so that it turned black before transportation. It could only be reconstituted into gold by the reverse process. However, despite the availability of this process for the transmutation of matter, the transmutation of base metals into gold through changes in their atomic structure was not possible.

**TRAVIS** – Space Commander, Alpha 15105. He lost his left arm and eye in a battle with Blake's Freedom Party, Blake himself causing the injury. Servalan appointed him Senior Executive Officer and gave him the task of seeking out and destroying Blake. At the time, he was under suspension pending an enquiry into the massacre of 1417 unarmed civilians on Auros and was generally recognised to be psychotic. He was later tried, dishonourably dismissed from the Service and sentenced to death, but he escaped and was finally killed by Avon after betraying the entire human race to the Andromedans.

**TRONOS** – Member of the Federation Space Assault Force on Albian. It was Tronos who initiated the countdown to destroy the planet after the Albians had broken through the Force's defences.

**TYCE** – Daughter of, and aide to, President Sarkoff of Lindor.

**TYNUS** – Commander on Fosforon and old friend of Avon, with whom he trained and subsequently worked a fraud.

**THE ULTRA** – The three custodians of Ultraworld. Apart from gathering knowledge, the Ultra were also charged with the responsibility of looking after the living centre of Ultraworld – the Core.

**ULTRASONIC FUSES** – Way of triggering bombs. The fuses were activated by sound and vibration.

**ULTRAWORLD** – Artificial planet with no electromagnetic spectrum reading due to a surface shielding that stopped all radiation leakage. The purpose of Ultraworld was to gather and process information and thus allow the Core to grow. It was described by Avon as the greatest accumulation of information in the known systems. The Ultra spoke of it as alive, feeding as it did off the brains and bodies of humanoids and other species they had collected for it.

**UNITED PLANETS** – Grouping of planets, dating from pre-Federation days, whose scientists built an artificial world that eventually turned up within Delta 714, code name Terminal.

**UNITED PLANETS OF TEAL** – Administrative union outside the Federation. Co-signatory of the Teal-Vandor Convention.

**UNMODIFIED** – Word used by mutoids to describe a human who had not been changed to a mutoid.

**URSA PRIME** – Location of Federation slave pits.

**USHTON** – Blake's father's brother. Ushton had a daughter Inga of whom Blake was very fond.

**UTILISER** – Code name used by Servalan in dealings with Cancer.

**VALERIA OF PRIM** – Slave bidder who used a proxy on Domo.

**VAMPIRES** – Name used by opponents of mutoid modification to describe mutoids.

**VANDOR CONFEDERACY** – Administrative union outside the Federation. Co-signatories to the Teal Vandor Convention.

**VARGAS** – Ruler of Cygnus Alpha.

**TEL VARON** – Blake's defence lawyer at his second trial. He was murdered on the orders of Dev Tarrant after he had discovered that the charges, and the trial, were fixed.

**VEM** – Unit of currency on Domo.

**VERLIS** – Slave saleswoman on Domo.

**VERON** – Daughter of Kasabi.

**VETIZADE** – Drink favoured by Travis on Freedom City.

**VETNOR** – Technical assistant to the rebel forces on Albian.

**VILA RESTAL** – Native of Earth, and brilliant picker of locks. He met Blake whilst waiting for transportation to Cygnus Alpha and promptly stole his watch. Despite the fact that he acted like a fool, Vila had a very high IQ and claimed to have bought his Delta grading in order to avoid becoming a Space Captain and hence killed. He was first sent to a penal colony at the age of fourteen, but the transportation ship was hit by a meteoroid and he escaped. Although Vila was in many respects a coward, he would not leave another member of the crew to die unless the action was out of sight, the odds against him high, and the bottle close to hand. Hence he risked his own life rescuing Tarrant on Terminal, but failed to help Cally on Obsidian. The nearest he ever came to having a true friend after he became connected with Blake was in Gan, whose straightforward bravery and strength he trusted. However, despite the contempt with which Avon and Vila regarded each other's characters, they subsequently became the closest of all crew members, each recognising the other's exceptional skills and abilities. This was seen at its clearest in episodes such as 'Killer' and 'Gambit' in Series B.

**VILA–WORLD** – Name given by Kerril to the planet to which she and Vila were instantaneously transported from Keezarn.

**VILKA** – Frontier world on which climate control broke down before the main attack on Star One.

**VINNI** — Android that became First Champion of the Vandor Confederacy. It killed Deeta Tarrant.

**VIRN** – The green planet on which it never rained. The sand that covered the planet was alive and sentient, and lived on human cellular tissue.

**VISPLAY** – Visual part of a communication from one computer to another.

**VISTAPES** – Means of inter-planetary communication used by private individuals within the Federation.

**VISUAL-IMAGE STRUCTURALISER** – Item used by Servalan to re-programme Avon's thoughts and make him think that he had actually seen Blake on Terminal.

**VORAY SCAN** – Method of scanning brain patterns, used on Gan when his brain limiter malfunctioned.

**WANDERER CLASS SPACE SHIP** (Initial Reference) – First space ships to reach deep space, 700 years before the time of Blake.

**WANDERER CLASS SPACE SHIP** (Second Reference) – A type of planet-hopper. Scorpio was a Mark II.

**WANTA** – After Helotrix, planet that was to be the follow-up to the Federation's experiments in re-colonisation.

**WAR CRIME STATUTE CODE** – Code under which Travis was tried and convicted.

**WARDIN** – Crew member of K47 Wanderer Class I space ship. He came back to life after 700 years and killed Dr Wiler.

**THE WEB** – A silica-based organic material similar to a fungus, used by the Auronar exiles to trap the Liberator. The spores generated rapidly and had great tensile strength. It was described as a line of genetic research that got out of control.

**WHITE DWARF** – Type of star of which Star One was an example. When most stars exhaust their nuclear material they collapse to about the size of Earth and, to all intents and purposes, die.

**WHITE MOUNTAINS** – An area on Helotrix some distance from the Magnetrix Terminal and thus outside the immediate concern and influence of the Federation occupying forces.

**DOCTOR WILER** – Doctor on Fosforon who performed an autopsy on the 700-year-old man from the K47 Wanderer Class ship.

**XARANOR** – Planet specialised in building and manning Federation exploration ships.

**X-BAR** – Federation penal colony for Grade IV offenders, visited by Blake many years previous to his capture of the Liberator. Travis took Inga hostage on it after it was abandoned by the Federation. It had a breathable atmosphere at low altitudes and a minimum of vegetation.

**XENON** – Planet in a star system outside of Federation control which Dorian used as a base. It was the home planet of the warring Seskas and Hommiks, and after Dorian's death was taken by Avon and the others as their final base. The base was destroyed through a series of controlled explosions after Scorpio departed on its last journey to Gauda Prime.

**XK 14** – Federation repair and supply base planet for deep-space cruisers. Blake planned to attack it after Cally was lost in the raid on Centero.

**XK 72** – Space laboratory with permanent research facilities financed by a research consortium of neutral planets. Avon had considered going to XK 72 should the situation aboard Liberator become impossible for him. It was destroyed by the Federation during an attack on Liberator.

**XX CODE** – Federation code indicating that nothing relating to the matter in question should be recorded in any form.

**ZEE** – A patient of Docholli whose leg was rebuilt by the surgeon.

**ZEE** – Hitech bounty hunter on Chenga. No connection with Zee above.

**ZEEONA** – Daughter of President Zukan of Betafarl. She was a biogenetic engineer who travelled to Xenon to be with Tarrant, whom she loved. She died at the base trying to remove the virus her father had implanted there.

**ZELDA** – Cally's twin. She was killed when Servalan destroyed the Replication Plant on Auron.

**ZEN** – Master computer on Liberator, with all guidance, battle and other secondary computers working under it. Zen was susceptible to influence by outside computers, such as Orac and the computers of the System. It finally broke down after being attacked by the fluid particles encounted en route for Terminal.

**ZEPHRON** – Home planet of Gan.

**ZEROK** – Frontier world outside the Federation (known as the Gold Planet), on which was housed a secret processor for the transmutation of gold into black matter and back again. It sold its gold to the Federation and to other places.

**ZETA 3 PARTICLES** – See Hyper Space Sub-Beam.

**ZIL** – Mischievous imp-like creature met by Blake in his retreat after the death of Gan.

**ZOLAF 4** – Planet on which Jenna and Tarvin undertook a smuggling operation in the course of which Jenna saved Tarvin's life.

**ZONDAR** – Planet that was the natural habitation of Moon Discs.

**ZONDAWL** – Planet ruled by Zykan.

**ZONDOR** – Planet on which the Federation's Pacification Programme was used just a few weeks prior to Avon's final meeting with Blake.

**ZONES** – The galaxy and surrounding space were divided into 10 general Zones, similar to the Quadrants and Sectors, but without subdivisions.

**ZONE 8** – Zone of space far beyond the normal reaches of the Federation and outside the normal trade lanes. It was on the edge of one of the two spiral arms.

**ZONE 9** – Zone of space beyond one of the spiral arms of the galaxy.

**ZUKAN** – President of Betafarl. Described variously as a pirate and an outlaw.

# The Fan Clubs and Bibliography

## AVON FAN CLUB

1 Elm Grove, Hildenborough, Tonbridge, Kent. Paul Darrow society producing newsletter four times a year and a variety of stickers, posters etc.

## BLAKE'S 7

205/211 Kentish Town Road, London NW5. Monthly comic published by Marvel Comics and available through newsagents. It contains a wide variety of photos taken on location during the filming of Series D, interviews, comic strip action, and stories.

## BLAKE'S 7 SWOP AND BUY FAN CLUB

Anthony King, 30 Midlothian St, Clayton, Manchester M11 4EP. Wide variety of Blake items available; no membership charges.

## FRONTIER WORLDS

Peter Lovelady, 2 Broadoaks Road, Sale, Cheshire M33 1SR. 'Blake's 7' and 'Dr Who' magazine, published four times per year.

# HORIZON

Sharon Eckman, 48 Gresham Gardens, Golders Green, London NW11. 'Blake's 7' appreciation society publishing a detailed newsletter/magazine four times a year. Full range of photos and other publications available.

# IMIPAC

Chris Clark, 111 Morley Hill, Enfield, Middx. Avon, Vila, Zen and Orac appreciation society publishing regular newsletter. Also has available a number of quality colour photos.

# LIBERATOR POPULAR FRONT

5 Bledlow House, Capland Street, London NW8 8RU. Largest 'Blake's 7' fan club in Britain. Publishes story summaries and four newsletters a year. Also a wide range of merchandise available.

# SCORPIO'S SEVEN

Michael Chambers, 1 Limbrick Avenue, Fairfield, Stockton, Cleveland TS19 7BZ. 'Blake's 7' fan club publishing four newsletters a year. A wide range of merchandise available.

# STANDARD BY SEVEN

38 Stephens Firs, Mortimer, Nr Reading, Berks. Very high quality amateur 'Blake's 7' magazine printed on offset litho – print run 500. Includes fan fiction, art etc. No back issue service available.

## TARIAL CELL

Frontier Worlds, 2 Broadoaks Road, Sale, Cheshire M33 1SR. 'Blake's 7' information publication.

## VILAWORLD

Secretary: Brenda Callagher, 195 Radipole Lane, Southill, Weymouth, Dorset DT4 0TQ. Vila/Michael Keating fan club; newsletter four times a year.

## THE BLAKE'S 7 BOOKS

'Blake's 7' by Trevor Hoyle, Sphere 1977.
'Project Avalon' by Trevor Hoyle, Arrow 1979.
'Scorpio Attack' by Trevor Hoyle, BBC 1981.

# Interviews

## VERE LORRIMER – Producer and Director

I was working for David Maloney when he became the first producer of 'Blake's 7', and he asked me if I would direct for him. I was very enthusiastic, because it was the first time the BBC had ever done a really full-length serial of this nature. I directed four episodes in each of the first three series. Then when the management decided to do a fourth series, David Maloney was producing something else so they had to find somebody to produce it, and as I was the most experienced hand at the game and still enjoyed it thoroughly I was offered the post, which I gladly took.

Although I had not been involved in science fiction before, I have done every conceivable type of work in television. I started in the presentation of three or four minute items to fill in time between programmes in the days before commercial television, when programmes didn't necessarily run to time at all. I graduated to dramatic children's programmes, and then into light entertainment and producing 'This is Your Life'. I directed an enormous number of comedy shows, such as 'Eric Sykes', and then started doing 'Dixon of Dock Green', directing more episodes of 'Dixon' than anybody did over a period of something like ten years. I did innumerable episodes of 'Z Cars' and 'Softly, Softly', and I became closely identified with police and action dramas.

In making the final series of 'Blake's 7' the first thing I

did was to visit Terry Nation in the USA where he was working at Columbia Pictures. We talked about the main theme, and we decided that the heroes no longer could run scared. They'd always been in retreat, firing shots backwards as they went. We decided that now they'd lost Blake, whether they liked it or not, attack was their only defence.

I then went to Chris Boucher and took his advice about authors. Inevitably we chose a mix – some people who'd done it very well in the past and would like to try again, and one or two new authors who'd never done it before so we could get some new ideas and new approaches. Every author writes a little differently – he wouldn't have his own individuality if he didn't – so Chris was able to take all these individual stories and amend them in little ways here and there to keep them true to the characteristics of the main players as they had developed over the series. The story would be altered, planed, until finally we had 125 pages of slick script with a lot of humorous lines in it, because fun and humour is part of the essence of a Blake script.

The director would then immediately start working on the script. For example, if you've got the heroes in a diamond mine that blows up, then you've got to build a mine somewhere or other, and you've got to plant the explosives and practise all that type of thing. There are three separate sections here – the filming of exteriors, the filming of special effects, and the interior scenes in the studios. Now the director casts all the guest artists as they are in each episode, and starts rehearsing them and filming them and recording them.

My role as producer, however, was mainly to guide and encourage and particularly to handle the publicity, including all the public relations work with the fan clubs and the hundreds and hundreds of letters that were received – and nobody has gone unanswered. As to the letters, there are those from people who are thrilled and delighted with it all. There are some people who are very,

very expert indeed at science fiction and pick holes in it all the time, because it's not scientific enough or things like that, or suggest all manner of ways of doing it which are way beyond anybody's budget. Then there's a whole category of people who have splendid ideas and offer stories verging from a page or two to whole scripts as long as 60, 70 or 80 pages. And of course we do have a number of people who regard it, for their own reasons, as outrageous that characters should be seen shooting and killing people – the fact that it's just like cowboys and Indians is quite beside the point to them.

The development of Avon as a personality came through discussion of the scripts, because we knew from the very start how it was going to end and it became clear to me that to make this work in a convincing way it was necessary for Avon to gradually become hyper-tense. Years and years of fighting, fighting, fighting with his life on the line had produced symptoms of paranoia. So in effect he was becoming more and more overbearing, and very hard to live with indeed. Many times the crew would have liked to have left him, but the fate they would find on stepping outside the ship would be worse than taking a chance with Avon.

But at the end there certainly was a way out. A group of people who become as real as Blake and the others can't really be extinguished, because they go on in your mind, in your imagination, in legend. So we didn't want them to go off into the distant galaxies, disappearing into further adventures as such, because after all that was how most episodes ended. We had to do something quite different, and we decided that it had to end in a way that nobody would ever forget. But at the same time the characters could survive – and indeed my correspondence has shown it, because I must have had about thirty different ideas of how they can be resuscitated – we left a clear loophole so that if the management ever decided to do the story again, it could indeed continue. But if in fact it was to be the end, we are left with them going on in legend in our mind's eye. Maybe they're killed, maybe they're not. Just like the Sundance Kid.

# CHRIS BOUCHER – Script Editor and Writer

It was my work on 'Dr Who' and coincidence that led me to Blake. David Maloney had just been appointed producer, and he's done rather more 'Dr Who' than anybody else. He was looking for an editor and I was looking for work, and the two just came together.

At its broadest and most basic, the script editor is responsible for getting scripts in an acceptable, practicable form, on time, and he or she does whatever is necessary to achieve that. Once you move into a series, you commission, you look for people who can do it, you discuss stories, you get them to do it.

Although I've been reading science fiction since I was a kid, it's just one genre I read. I get a little nervous with people who totally and exclusively focus down on one particular area of fiction or drama, because they get single-minded. I actually think – I might seem pompous now – that any genre actually benefits by having fed into it influences from other areas. Some of Asimov's best things for me are whodunits. I don't dislike crossing genre barriers.

Doing Blake rapidly became, in practical terms, about survival. It was about getting enough material to feed the monster. The problem with a series is that you can't feed in too many semi-variables because every time, for example, you introduce a character who becomes a regular or a semi-regular you're into expense and logistical problems. Actors don't want to tie themselves up for six months on the basis that they're going to appear in four episodes. With the sort of system that we're using where you do the main video part of the show in the Television Centre and you do location film inserts at a different time, it means that you are filming, say, over a month and the guys who have appeared on film won't appear in the studio for another six weeks, which means you've got to book them in and it all gets so complicated that even when you've got a very good character you hesitate because you know you're going to give yourself a hell of a lot of problems if you bring him back!

Many of my scripts were written because there were holes left within the progression of stories. If there was a gap for one of the characters – let's say one of the regulars hadn't had a strong episode in a series – then I would write that one.

As to Blake himself, over the last three episodes of Series B I was trying to show the problem of a lot of revolutionary leaders, from Zapata on down, that in sustaining that sort of life, that sort of pressure, they are inevitably changed. And I felt that it was reaching a point where we had to make some sort of statement about what was happening to the man – he had killed a lot of people, he had blown a lot of things up – his motives frequently might have been impeccable, but I mistrust clear blacks and clear whites and I was conscious that having reached that stage, he'd either got to be stupid, and he wasn't, or he'd got to be fanatical. And so I just nudged him a little further towards the fanatical end of the scale. I thought it was time for him to start questioning himself, to feel a little less certain about what he was doing.

The Federation did very nasty things and they dressed in black and they wore death masks, but basically, as in any dictatorship, it didn't actually touch a large proportion of the population – and I felt Blake had to be aware of this. He had to reach a point where he understood that if he actually got the opportunity to destroy the Federation he'd have to kill an awful lot of people to do it. The line between the freedom fighter and the terrorist is a fairly thin one, and it's one I would've thought Robin Hood and others like him had to stumble up to occasionally and ask whether what they were doing was really what they should be doing.

Avon on the other hand had a vested interest in the status quo which Blake didn't have. Again, what I hoped would come out of the end of the second series and what I tried to feed into the later series was that we all have to have some sort of creed to hang on to, even a psychopath which I think he was really. Avon's crutch was personal loyalty, when it came down to it, and Blake turned out to be one of the few people he looked towards. I found their parting quite touching, and I felt Blake's estimate of Avon's real character – 'For what it's worth, I've always trusted you from the beginning' – was absolutely correct. I think Avon never actually did half of what he said. He bad-mouthed far more than he actually did.

Towards the end of the last season, I was moving Avon in the same direction as Blake had gone. There was always an ambiguity with Avon, there was always the possibility that he was doing it out of self-interest, or he could've been doing it out of altruism. Inside every cynic there's an idealist desperately yearning to be let out, and when they are let out they're usually a real pain and cause all sorts of trouble. Avon was left with one ideal human being, one ideal of certainty, and that was Blake. He then found himself in a situation where Blake appeared to have betrayed him, and he couldn't take it. He understood computer systems and machines much more readily than he did people.

But with Vila there was a 'one man and his dog' sort of routine. They were two practical men in their way. In some way Avon saw himself as Vila writ large. Avon had an affection for him, but it was not the affection of equals – he saw Vila very much as a character he could understand and therefore control. There was no doubt about Vila in his mind, though there was doubt with an awful lot of other people, including Tarrant. There was no doubt in his mind, actually, about Blake. He really believed the guy was honest. He had believed the same of Anna Grant but she let him down totally.

As to the very end of the final series, I offered it expecting somebody to say no, hang on, one or two can go down but not all of them – and nobody did. But apart from Blake, none of them are necessarily dead. Certainly if the thing came back, the ones who want to do it again aren't dead and the ones who don't want to do it again are.

## PAUL DARROW – Avon

I felt from the beginning that Avon was a much more interesting character, potentially, than a lot of the others. That implies no disrespect to the other characters, but I always think it's very difficult to play the straight-up-and-down heroes of the sort Gareth Thomas had to play. He had to be thoroughly moral all the time – he couldn't shoot anybody in the back, he couldn't hit a woman, he couldn't do an unpleasant thing or think an unpleasant thought. And of course, life isn't like that. So I wanted to play Avon as realistically as possible within the science fiction element, push him out a bit, and fortunately Terry Nation and Chris Boucher gave me the OK.

I determined to play him in a 'Dirty Harry' way all the way through, however long the series went on. But I felt that towards the end of the second series, one of us really had to go. I thought it could be me or it could be Blake. But the Avon character is one that you can put into all sorts of circumstances which you couldn't put the Blake character in, because Avon was always unpredictable. He could just as easily turn round and kill Blake as he would turn round and kill somebody else. That was the fascination of the character for me and perhaps provoked the interest that I have had in the character from other people.

Through the series I wanted to show more and more that this man, with all the attributes of a winner (and all along the line he is a winner – he is the only one left standing at the end) really deserved to be the loser. And in order to play it, I needed to give it the realism. If you're the man in a white hat and shining armour and you're always going to win, you're Superman, and that's fun . . . but it gets boring after 50 episodes. What people like to see, I think, is somebody realistic in an unrealistic situation, where they can believe that a man would have to behave like that.

What Avon had to do was become his own man, and he never could while Blake was around. Blake had to be removed, so I deliberately played the character in such a way that whoever wrote that last episode would be forced to either kill off Avon or have some kind of confrontation. What I thought would happen was that I would be killed in the end!

What would have been very interesting and much more believable perhaps right from the beginning – in fact it happened in the end – was to make Blake much more like Avon. As one of the guest actors once said to me, ' "Blake's 7" is the only programme on television where a right bastard is the hero.'

I felt that Avon would find it amusing that fate was the only thing that could defeat him. He was in fact unbeatable anywhere else – often because he fought dirty. So that was why, at the end of the third series when Liberator was lost and Servalan tricked him, I had Avon smile. What else could he do?

However by the third series there were occasions when Avon did things which I thought were quite out of character for him – like not killing enemies when he had the chance. I pointed this out but was told, 'We think now that Blake's gone you ought to be a little more moral'. I didn't like that, which is why I went as far as I did in the fourth series, because I thought, I'm not letting them make Avon into another Blake, he's got to be real all the way through.

On the other hand the relation between Avon and Vila

worked tremendously. Both Michael and I were very disappointed that that wasn't developed more than it was. The best writer for us was Robert Holmes, and he got that relationship perfectly. Whenever we heard a Bob Holmes script was coming up we didn't even bother to read it, we knew it would be good. Avon tolerates Vila, he's no threat you see, but he could be useful in opening the odd safe. Tarrant, however, was treated as cannon fodder. Tarrant was always saying, 'I'm going to go out there with a gun and face this guy,' and Avon would say, 'Go ahead, go ahead,' because while the guy's shooting at Tarrant Avon can slip around the back and get him, and if Tarrant gets killed as well, hard luck. But the opportunity rarely arose with Vila, because Vila never volunteered for anything.

I think the BBC could probably have got another series out of it if they wanted to. It would be very interesting to see who they allowed to survive. Avon is last seen standing, so presumably he could survive. Servalan is not dead as far as we know. Orac is still around somewhere. So you've now got two of the original seven, plus the baddy. I don't know whether they'd want to do that. And maybe Vila wasn't killed, maybe he was just wounded . . . It would be a little ludicrous though if none of them were killed. Blake, however, was killed properly. Gareth wanted to be absolutely certain he was dead – it was in his contract – and the only way you can do that is with blood. That was why it was a different type of gun, not a laser. But Avon was left standing, he's still there. . .

## MICHAEL KEATING – Vila

After going to the Guildhall School of Music and Drama, I got a job as an assistant stage manager, had various theatre roles, and eventually in 1971 did my first telly for the BBC, for Pennant Roberts. About once a year after that I used to work for Pennant in different productions for the BBC in between theatre jobs. Then in '77 when I had finished with the National Theatre he offered me four episodes in 'Dr Who', and that actually led to 'Blake's 7'. Pennant put my name forward to David Maloney, and I went along to see him. At that time they hadn't really got round to thinking of what sort of character they wanted for Vila, and apparently when I walked in David thought that I was the man for the job.

I felt an immediate empathy for the role. The thing about it was there wasn't a hell of a lot to go on in the first four episodes and I always got the feeling that the writers were watching us and seeing how we developed the characters. The writers would pick on certain things that we were doing and they would use them. For instance, early on in the first series, we overran on a lot of the episodes with the result that we were working quite long days, and in between shots I would have a little snooze. Then they actually began to write it into the script that Vila would be quite sleepy. I also once said to Chris Boucher that my daughter watched the series and had turned around to me one time and said, 'Daddy, you're stupid'. Chris then thought he'd write me an episode where I actually got the girl and was quite brave – this was in 'City at the Edge of the World'.

The interaction between Vila and Avon was of course in the script, but also we were great mates and this made it work particularly well. Having a very cold, calculating character and someone who is rather vulnerable and full of flaws was a good idea. Vila was always very necessary to the story because he had the talent of opening locks. Otherwise, I think Avon would have chucked him off the ship earlier. He was a great survivor.

At the end of the fourth series, I suddenly did a bit of karate and knocked that young girl out. I always said to Chris, 'Look, if Vila's in a tight spot I think he should show that he can defend himself, if it really comes to the crunch,' and I'm glad he used it. On the other hand, in

'Orbit' when I was hiding from Avon, we had arranged that I would be crying, because he was the one guy that I needed for my survival and there he was trying to kill me. And in fact when I was hiding I actually had tears. But the powers that be decided that that was 'too real', they didn't think it was right for the series and they cut it. There is a slight sob, but that's all. You still don't know whether I'm sweating or what.

After that episode, Vila never really relates to Avon again, he becomes very, very wary of him. Vila didn't become a paranoid schizophrenic like Avon did, he was just interested in surviving. Which may be me as well. As an actor, I don't particularly want to be a big star, I just want to carry on in the business playing as many different parts as I can and taking it as it comes.

As to the end of the series, perhaps I should have died in Episode 11 and fallen out of the ship, but then I suppose Paul would've lost all his fans! When the series did end I had a lot of letters from people saying how upset they were, including some from people who had been out of work for months and seeing that episode just before Christmas really made them suicidal, which I felt bad about. Perhaps it was the wrong timing to have put it on just before Christmas, especially with the continuing confusion between good and evil. If we were supposed to be the good guys, evil won, although if you worked it out, the Federation weren't that bad. There were independent planets that seemed to get on quite happily, and we seemed to go around disturbing them.

If Vila did survive the final shoot-out he would try and get off that planet somehow. He's not a pilot, so maybe he'd stow away in a hold. He'd certainly get out of that area and try and find somewhere else to live. He probably would be caught after a time and would play dumb and end up working for the Federation for a bit, then seeing an opportunity to escape, perhaps try to find Kerril . . . .

# PETER TUDDENHAM – Zen, Orac, Slave

In playing Zen, Orac and Slave I gave what I thought would be an interpretation of the lines as I saw the characters. For Zen the producers didn't want a Dalek type, they wanted something which was almost human but not quite. So that's what I produced. When Orac came along at the end of Series A, it was originally intended that I was going to take Orac as Derek had done it. He had a not dissimilar voice from mine in normal speaking, and although he didn't give Orac a very big character, he did give it that bit of edge, of irascibility. I listened to the tapes of him and I copied it to the best of my ability. Then I put my own personality into it and made it a bit faster.

As to Slave, Chris Boucher invented the character to be a bit obsequious, and I read the lines and gave what I thought might be a reading. Chris and Vere seemed to like it – a Uriah Heep type of character I think. I really wanted three completely different characters, and it seemed to work.

'Blake's 7' was a new adventure for me. I had done a few computer voices for 'Dr Who' about seven or eight years ago, and I'm still getting little tiny cheques from repeats in Hawaii and things. But I had never done anything quite like this before. With Zen and Orac and Slave I liked to play the character live – even when Orac and Zen were in the same scene. Once I virtually answered myself. I love doing that. I used to record one of the voices occasionally if things got too complicated but I hate to record the whole lot in the studio and not be a part of the action. I had my monitor and my headphones on and could see what was going on, and I took my cue from the actors. And the lovely part was I didn't have to learn anything!

Historically I am a theatre actor if the opportunity comes along. But I have concentrated more on radio and television over recent years. I've done a lot of light comedy and farce in leading parts – I've toured, I've done the West End in revue, I've touched nearly every branch of the business. For example I worked with Noel Coward, and I worked for Peter Hall on the film of 'Akenfield' in which I played, again unseen, the character of the old grandfather talking to his son. That was a big success and won all sorts of awards and brought me quite a bit of work.

I have come to specialise in accents, particularly the Suffolk, East Anglian accent, and I dialect advise a lot on television plays set in the country there. And since Blake I have done a lot of commercials as well as training films for various companies, often involving computer voices. My main science fiction work however has been in radio plays. I recently played the lead in 'The Reluctant Cecil', a matinee about an 89-year-old incontinent computer, a marvellous part. But I don't want to be stuck with computers all my life. In fact I had never thought of playing computers until Vere Lorrimer rang me up and said they wanted a voice, and would I go along.

One thing it has all meant is a lot of fan mail. Some very earnest schoolboys have been asking me all sorts of very intricate scientific questions which I couldn't possibly answer, but they think I am the computer and I should know! I pass those letters on to Terry Nation or the writers. After the third series when Zen was blown up in the ship, I had a letter from a woman who said what a marvellous character I made of Zen and how upset she was that he died – her little girl couldn't sleep afterwards and cried over Zen saying, 'I failed you'. Then when I went to a convention last year a little girl in a wheelchair asked how I felt when Zen died. I said I was upset to see the character go, but you have to play your part and that's it. I went down to speak to her later and found this was the same little girl who had cried all night when Zen died. I had had no idea that she was a cripple. It was very moving for me.

# Conclusion – Towards More Adventures

Each series of 'Blake's 7' ended with a catastrophe. In Series A it appeared that the newly captured Orac was predicting the destruction of Liberator (in fact it was an identical sister ship that blew up).

Series B saw the Liberator survive, but with Blake seriously injured and the rest of the crew facing the oncoming alien invasion fleet with little chance of survival. They did survive of course, but not without the ship sustaining severe damage.

Series C saw the end of Liberator and the crew stuck on Terminal with some very inhospitable animals and plants for company.

Finally, Series D finished on Gauda Prime with a big shoot-out and more of the heroes appearing to end up dead than alive.

But of course it need not end there. Even if there is to be no more 'Blake's 7' on television, there are hundreds of possible continuations which can be worked out. Indeed the BBC have already been swamped by possible scripts, and the fanzines are full of possibilities.

Therefore, for anyone who fancies working out a continuation of the story, here is a rundown on the state of the main characters, as at the end of Episode 52.

**AVON:** Alive – possibly totally paranoid after the shock of his betrayal by Anna Grant and the constant long-term exposure to danger and death, and quite probably no longer even sure where his own interests lie. But nonetheless alive, and a prisoner of Federation guards on Gauda Prime.

**BLAKE:** Dead – shot by Avon in the final episode. Even though Blake's behaviour on Gauda Prime was, to say the least, odd (considering his previous desire to hit the Federation on Earth, it was a strange place from which to launch a revolution), there is no doubt that Avon killed him. There is a Blake clone quite possibly still alive and living with the freed slave girl Rashel on an unnamed planet and guarding the Imipak weapon. There was also a hint that Clonemaster Fen had produced a third Blake clone (in addition to the one shot by Travis) which could be lurking around somewhere.

**CALLY:** Dead – killed on Terminal during the explosions set by Servalan. Avon verified her death, having gone back down the shaft to look for her and Orac.

**DAYNA:** ??? If the guns used on the Gauda Prime shoot-out had bullets in them, Dayna, Tarrant and Soolin were either killed or seriously injured. If not perhaps they were stunned. There is one precedent for Federation guards using weapons without the intention to kill – in Project Avalon, where part of the plot was to let Blake and the others escape capture whilst thinking they had in fact rescued Avalon. Perhaps the guards were trying to take them all in for a bounty (as Blake himself suggested to Tarrant), or perhaps they were not Federation Guards at all or had something more complex in mind . . . .

**GAN:** Dead – killed on Earth by an explosion created by Travis during the raid on Control.

**JENNA:** Reported dead by Blake to Tarrant, having returned to her old smuggler's ways after leaving Liberator. However Blake was testing Tarrant at the time, and may have used the name and story just to see if he would get any reaction. After all, Zen had never linked her location after the Intergalactic War with that of Blake, and there is no reason to suppose Blake really knew what had happened to her.

**ORAC:** Still working – Orac travelled with Avon and the others to Gauda Prime and was used by Avon on the planet until the final scene, when it was suddenly no longer to be seen. Hence Avon had presumably hidden Orac away somewhere safe pending any disaster. It is also worth remembering that Ensor, the inventor of Orac, had a number of brilliant students who might also have been capable of building an Orac or Orac variant.

**SERVALAN:** Alive – not seen since her disastrous attempt to use Egrorian to steal Orac and gain the Tachyon Funnel. Last heard of still using the name Commissioner Sleer and still desperate to regain her old power base within the Federation.

**SLAVE:** Badly damaged (but not destroyed) during the landing on Gauda Prime. A computer expert could rebuild Slave, especially with the help of Orac. It is also possible that other versions of Slave were built by Dorian and could have survived the explosions on Xenon base.

**SOOLIN:** ??? See Dayna.

**TARRANT:** ??? See Dayna. It is worth remembering that Tarrant was already seriously injured through the crash of Scorpio and so was liable to drop at any moment, shot or no shot.

**TRAVIS:** Dead – killed by Avon on Star One.

**VILA:** ??? After disarming the Federation officer Arlen following Avon's killing of Blake, Vila hit the floor at the sound of the first shot from a Federation weapon, despite the fact that no-one was seen firing at him. Did he drop in fear or was he shot, and if shot was the weapon deadly or just on stun?

**ZEN:** Extinguished with the Liberator whilst in orbit around Terminal. The sister ship DSV1 (presumably with another Zen on board) was destroyed by Orac, although there may have been a DSV3 built by the System. As the System was destroyed during the visit of Liberator, it is possible that any other DSVs with Zens on board would be roaming freely through the galaxy.

Finally of course there is always the possibility of brothers and sisters of leading characters appearing, perhaps seeking revenge. The only crew members for whom we have definite knowledge of siblings are:

**AVON:** A brother. No details ever given, but he was obviously important to Avon, as Zen projected a picture of him as a defence mechanism when Liberator was first boarded. Presumably alive.

**DAYNA:** Adopted sister killed by the Sarrans.

**TARRANT:** Brother killed when First Champion of Teal.

So much for the characters, but what of the situation? How did it change during the existence of 'Blake's 7'? In many respects, there was no change. The Federation existed much as before, and the Intergalactic War and destruction of Star One had a far greater impact than the crews of Scorpio and Liberator. On the negative side, a number of good people died following their involvement with Blake and/or Avon: Nova, Hal Mellanby, Dr Plaxton . . . .

Of course 'Blake's 7' did kill off some nasty creatures

too — Travis, a number of Andromedans, the Ultra . . . .
But as for Servalan, there was an eternal stalemate. She
never got Orac or the Liberator, but she did get the Zerok
gold and succeeded in escaping death after being overthrown as President. Tarrant and Avon both had clear
chances to kill her, but let them go.

So all in all, there has been a lot of action and a lot of
deaths, but very little change. Indeed the Pylene 50
programme so closely resembled the drug-induced state
of the inhabitants of Earth shown at the start of series A
that one could be excused for thinking that nothing had
happened at all.

If the Federation was able to withstand the destruction
of 80% of its fleet and its most important computer base
and still go on expanding, then whatever it was that was
needed to make major changes would have to be either
incredibly big and strong, or so radical and unusual that
the main force at the disposal of the Federation (its sheer
size and single-minded brutality) could not resist it. The
plan, after Blake's life, would have to be something previously unthought-of if it was to change the Federation at
all. Something unique . . . .